God's big plan for Christ's new people

EPHESIANS

by Thabiti Anyabwile

D0967825

thegoodbook
COMPANY

God's big plan for Christ's new people
The Good Book Guide to Ephesians
© Thabiti Anyabwile/The Good Book Company, 2010. Reprinted 2010, 2014, 2015.
Series Consultants: Tim Chester, Tim Thornborough,
                    Anne Woodcock, Carl Laferton

The Good Book Company
Tel (UK): 0333 123 0880
Tel: (US): 866 244 2165
Email (UK): info@thegoodbook.co.uk
Email (US): info@thegoodbook.com

Websites
UK: www.thegoodbook.co.uk
North America: www.thegoodbook.com
Australia: www.thegoodbook.com.au
New Zealand: www.thegoodbook.co.nz

ISBN: 9781907377099

Printed in the Czech Republic

CONTENTS

Introduction: Good Book Guides

Every Bible-study group is different—yours may take place in a church building, in a home or in a cafe, on a train, over a leisurely mid-morning coffee or squashed into a 30-minute lunch break. Your group may include new Christians, mature Christians, non-Christians, mums and tots, students, businessmen or teens. That's why we've designed these *Good Book Guides* to be flexible for use in many different situations.

Our aim in each session is to uncover the meaning of a passage, and see how it fits into the "big picture" of the Bible. But that can never be the end. We also need to appropriately apply what we have discovered to our lives. Let's take a look at what is included:

⊕ **Talkabout:** Most groups need to "break the ice" at the beginning of a session, and here's the question that will do that. It's designed to get people talking around a subject that will be covered in the course of the Bible study.

⊥ **Investigate:** The Bible text for each session is broken up into manageable chunks, with questions that aim to help you understand what the passage is about. **The Leader's Guide** contains **guidance on questions**, and sometimes ⊗ additional "follow-up" questions.

⊡ **Explore more (optional):** These questions will help you connect what you have learned to other parts of the Bible, so you can begin to fit it all together like a jig-saw; or occasionally look at a part of the passage that's not dealt with in detail in the main study.

⊃ **Apply:** As you go through a Bible study, you'll keep coming across **apply** sections. These are questions to get the group discussing what the Bible teaching means in practice for you and your church. ⊡ **Getting personal** is an opportunity for you to think, plan and pray about the changes that you personally may need to make as a result of what you have learned.

⊤ **Pray:** We want to encourage prayer that is rooted in God's word—in line with his concerns, purposes and promises. So each session ends with an opportunity to review the truths and challenges highlighted by the Bible study, and turn them into prayers of request and thanksgiving.

The **Leader's Guide** and introduction provide historical background information, explanations of the Bible texts for each session, ideas for **optional extra** activities, and guidance on how best to help people uncover the truths of God's word.

Why study Ephesians?

"My Christian faith is really all about my personal relationship with Jesus."

"I can have church anywhere. I don't need to go to a building or be with a lot of people."

"My friends and I do church at our favourite coffee shop."

"Why should I join a local church? I'm a Christian so I'm part of the universal body of Christ. Isn't that enough?"

Perhaps you've heard comments like this before. Maybe this is how you're currently thinking about church. Today, many Christians view the Christian faith primarily in terms of individual or small-group activities; faith is a personal and a private matter. At best, church is something we do out of convenience, and at worst, it distorts what it means to be Christian. "Spiritual" experiences and beliefs are the important thing, but the concrete, gritty reality of living together as Christ's people is just an optional extra.

Paul, however, shows us a radically different view of church in his letter to the Ephesians. Not only is the church of Christ not an inconvenient extra, it is the display of God's wisdom to the universe! The church is God's handiwork, made up of people from every kind of background, living under the gracious rule of Christ Himself. As part of the church we are hand-selected by God through Christ so that, by being a new kind of community, we will show the world the mystery of God's electing love.

In short, Christianity is far more corporate and public than we might expect. We are redeemed individually, but we are placed in a family. Living out the Christian life means living together with others who love the same Lord. It means actively participating in the church, for the church is God's only plan to raise us to full maturity in Jesus Christ.

The ten sessions in this Good Book Guide will help us, as groups or individuals, to discover from Paul's letter the richness of God's grace in His church, and to grow as part of the body of Christ.

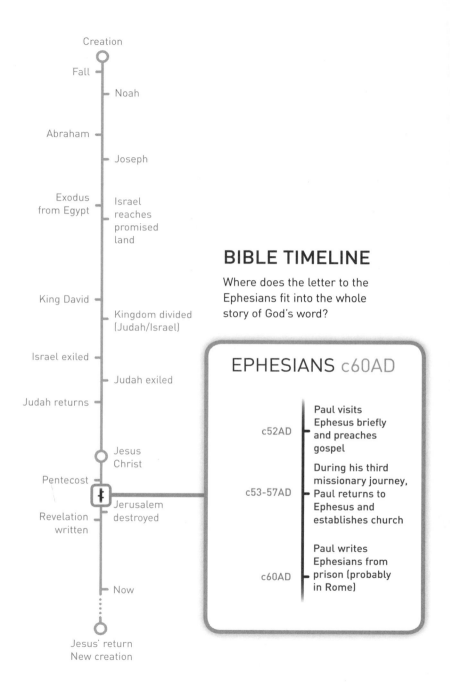

Creation

Fall

Noah

Abraham

Joseph

Exodus from Egypt

Israel reaches promised land

BIBLE TIMELINE

Where does the letter to the Ephesians fit into the whole story of God's word?

King David

Kingdom divided (Judah/Israel)

EPHESIANS c60AD

Israel exiled

Judah exiled

Judah returns

Jesus Christ

c52AD — Paul visits Ephesus briefly and preaches gospel

Pentecost

c53-57AD — During his third missionary journey, Paul returns to Ephesus and establishes church

Jerusalem destroyed

Revelation written

c60AD — Paul writes Ephesians from prison (probably in Rome)

Now

Jesus' return New creation

1

Ephesians 1 v 1-14
BLESSED IN CHRIST

⊕ **talkabout**

1. What words or phrases come to mind when you think of the word "church"?

⊕ **investigate**

The book of Acts includes an account of Paul's time in Ephesus, describing the remarkable beginning of the church there and giving us the historical background to this letter. As we will see, these dramatic events later came to be reflected in some of the themes of his letter.

▶ **Read Acts 19 v 1-20**

2. Who did Paul preach to in Ephesus (v 8-10)?

> **DICTIONARY**
>
> **Repentance (v 4):** turning away from sin.
> **Maligned (v 9):** criticised.
> **The Way (v 9):** Christianity.

3. Contrast the message that Paul brought to Ephesus with the beliefs already held by some there (v 1-6). What happened to those who accepted the message preached by Paul?

• How did people change when they accepted this message (v 17-20)?

4. What other responses were there (v 9, 13)?

▶ Read Acts 19 v 23-41

5. What was the reason for Demetrius' opposition (v 25-27), and what does this tell us about the new Ephesian Christians?

6. What was the city clerk's verdict on Paul and his colleagues (v 37)?

▶ Read Acts 20 v 17-38

7. Paul spent three years in Ephesus (v 31). What does verse 17 show had resulted from his time there?

❯ Read Ephesians 1 v 1-2

8. Who is this letter from, how is he described, and who is it addressed to?

- How should this shape our attitude to these studies?

⊡ **getting personal**

To receive a greeting like this should definitely make us pay close attention. Paul's words here in verses 1-2 are more than a throwaway greeting. They are trumpet blasts—a wake-up call blown in our ears—to wake us from our slumber to give attention to the word of the living God in the Scriptures.

How are you approaching these studies in Ephesians?

❯ Read Ephesians 1 v 3-14

9. What *exactly* does verse 3 tell us about the blessings that Christians receive from God? (When, where, how much and how?)

10. What does "every spiritual blessing" look like? To help you answer this question, fill in the table. (Note: We'll be looking at verses 4-14 in much more detail in Study Two.)

Verse	What is the blessing from God?	What else is said about this blessing?	What difference does it make? (complete in Study Two)
v 4		Who? When? For what?	
v 5		How? Why did God do this?	
v 6		How?	
v 7		How? What does that mean for us?	
v 8			
v 9-10		What is His will?	

Verse	What is the blessing from God?	What else is said about this blessing?	What difference does it make? (complete in Study Two)
v 11	"We were also chosen" (NIV) is better translated as "we have obtained an inheritance" (ESV).		
v 13a		When?	
v 13-14		What does the Holy Spirit do for us?	

11. In the first 14 verses of Ephesians, how many times is the phrase "in Christ" (including "in him" and "in the One he loves") used?

• What truth does this emphasise?

⊡ explore more

Paul frequently describes Christians as "in Christ". Union with Christ runs throughout Ephesians: when Paul discusses the inter-ethnic relationships of Jews and Gentiles (chapter 2), the mystery of marriage (chapter 5), and especially as he describes what it means to be saved.

> **Read Ephesians 1 v 13; 2 Corinthians 5 v 21; Galatians 2 v 20**

What details do we find here about what it means to be "in Christ"?

> **Read 1 Corinthians 6 v 14-20; 2 Corinthians 6 v 14-17**

What does this mean for us in practice?

⊟ apply

12. What troubles you at the moment—tempting you to question whether you can go on as a Christian?

• How does verse 3 help us in these troubles, temptations and questions?

⊡ getting personal

Whatever the thought, idea or feeling that makes you doubt you can be a faithful Christian, it is *lying* to you. "Every spiritual blessing in Christ" has already been given to you. Your life is blessed beyond anything that you have ever imagined. This is a gargantuan, colossal, staggering, dumbfounding, enormous truth! Get hold of it with all of your might and plan how you will start to live it out this week.

⊡ pray

Re-read Ephesians 1 v 3. Let everything you say to God now be shaped by this truth.

2 Ephesians 1 v 3-14
SAVED BY GOD

The story so far

Christ's people are those who have been blessed by God with every spiritual blessing in Christ.

⬌ talkabout

1. How confident are you that you are forgiven by God and that you will be saved from condemnation on the Day of Judgment? Do you change from day to day? If so, what increases your confidence, and what makes you sometimes doubt your salvation?

⬇ investigate

> **Read Ephesians 1 v 3-14**

2. God in three persons (the Trinity) is at work in saving us. What does each member of the Trinity specifically do in this work of saving us to become part of God's people?

- The Father (v 4-6):

- The Son (v 7-12):

- The Holy Spirit (v 13-14):

DICTIONARY

Predestined (v 5): chose the future for.
To sonship (v 5): as heir.
The One (v 6): Jesus Christ.
Redemption (v 7): the buying of someone's freedom at a cost.
In conformity (v 11): in line.
Deposit (v 14): an initial payment that guarantees the rest of the money will follow.

3. What is God's choice based on (v 4, 5, 11)?

God does not choose us because of some quality in us that deserves His attention, or because He saw who would believe and decided to choose them, or because of our works or good deeds. All of these ideas are popular with some people: but the Bible nowhere teaches them.

4. What does the word "adoption" (v 5) tell us about the change from our old way of life as unbelievers to our new life in Christ?

5. "Redemption" means being purchased out of slavery. What does this tell us about how our life changes when we are included in Christ?

6. A better translation of "we were also chosen" (v 11) is "we have obtained an inheritance" (ESV). What does this tell us, first about our life in this world and then our life in the future?

⊡ explore more

optional

In verse 14 Paul describes how the Holy Spirit has been given to Christians as "a deposit guaranteeing our inheritance" (see also 2 Corinthians 1 v 22). In Romans 8 he outlines what it means for us to have God's Spirit in our heart.

▸ Read Romans 8 v 5-28

List the characteristics of someone who has the Spirit.

⊡ apply

7. How can we know for certain if we have been saved or not? How might this Bible passage help you to help someone who is unsure that they are truly saved?

⊡ getting personal

Do you sometimes question whether or not you are truly saved? Assuming there's no unrepentant sin troubling your conscience, think about why you hope God will accept you as one of His people. Are you trying to base your confidence on anything other than what is written in verses 3-14? If so, you are trusting in the wrong things. Instead, rely on all that God has done for you in Christ.

⊡ investigate

8. What is the ultimate purpose of the saving work of God the Father, Son and Holy Spirit (v 6, 12, 14)?

9. How will God's great purpose ultimately be achieved (v 9-10)?

• How do you think the church fits into God's great plan?

10. What is Paul's response—and what should be ours—to the amazing truth that Christians have "every spiritual blessing in Christ" (v 3, 14)?

➡ apply

11. What does a lack of praising God in our lives show us about ourselves?

12. How should God's great purpose for our world shape your priorities in life? And those of your church?

⊡ getting personal

Think about the words in this Bible passage used to describe Christ's people (that's you, if you are in Christ)—chosen, predestined, adopted, redeemed, forgiven, included, marked, guaranteed... How will these truths make a difference in your life this week?

⬆ pray

Give thanks for all that each member of the Trinity has done in your life.

Pray that you would grow, not only in understanding of all that God has done for you, but also in love and trust towards your heavenly Father, in submission to Christ your Head and in the encouragement of the Holy Spirit.

3 Ephesians 1 v 15-23
EYES OPENED BY THE SPIRIT

The story so far

Christ's people are those who have been blessed by God with every spiritual blessing in Christ.

Christ's people have been saved by God—the Father, Son and Spirit—as part of God's great plan to bring everything in the universe under Christ's authority.

⊕ talkabout

1. Imagine meeting and getting to know people in a workplace or social group. How do you think you might recognise a true Christian? What characteristics would you expect to see?

⊕ investigate

▶ Read Ephesians 1 v 15-23

Paul begins: *"For this reason* ... I have not stopped giving thanks for you" (v 15-16), referring back to verses 3-14. In light of all that God—Father, Son, and Spirit—has done and is doing to redeem the Ephesian Christians for himself, Paul cannot help but give constant, delighted thanks to God for this church of saved sinners.

> **DICTIONARY**
>
> **Revelation (v 17):** being able to understand.
> **Enlightened (v 18):** able to see.
> **Rule and authority, power and dominion (v 21):** unseen spiritual forces.

2. What's the two-part definition of a true Christian or a genuine church given by Paul in verse 15?

⮕ apply

3. In light of Paul's definition, what's the problem with statements like: "I've got faith" or even: "I have faith in God"?

4. And what's the problem with being a lone Christian?

⬇ investigate

Paul's praise for God in verses 3-14 leads to his prayer for the Ephesian believers in verses 16-18.

5. Look at *how* Paul prays for the Ephesian Christians in verses 16-19. What principles can you find that should shape our prayers as well?

⮕ apply

6. How do our prayers for each other compare with Paul's example here?

▣ getting personal

How purposeful are your prayers? How often do you pray for the spiritual wellbeing of your Christian brothers and sisters? Or are you mostly focused on earthly matters? Aim to make your prayers this week reflect your love for all God's people and your faith in the Lord Jesus.

7. What does Paul pray for the Ephesian Christians in verse 17? Why?

8. Find three things in verses 18-19 that Paul wants Christians to know.

-
-
-

- How do we come to know these things?

9. If the Ephesian Christians already have "every spiritual blessing in Christ", why does Paul need to continually pray for their spiritual wellbeing, do you think?

10. Paul's prayers reveal another defining mark of true Christians (see v 17). What is it?

11. How do Christians now "see" Christ (v 20-21)?

12. Where does the church fit in God's great plan (v 22-23)?

optional

⊡ explore more

❯ **Read 1 Corinthians 1 v 18-25**

How do non-Christians view the message of Christ crucified? What kind of message do they want?

How do Christians view the message of Christ crucified? See also verse 30. What do you think makes the difference?

❯ **Read 1 Corinthians 2 v 1-5**

Paul's message and preaching came with "a demonstration of the Spirit's power" (v 5). What do you think that was?

⊖ apply

13. Non-believers don't have the Holy Spirit working in their lives. In what way, therefore, are they different from Christians?

• What difference will this make to our relationships with them?

14. What do the truths of verses 19-23 mean for:
• our personal discipleship?

• our stewardship of what God has given us?

• our church and its leadership/direction?

• our involvement in our society?

⊕ **pray**

"I have not stopped giving thanks for you, remembering you in my prayers."

Give thanks now for each other, for your church leaders, for those in your fellowship and for faithful Christians around the world.

Put into practice what you have learned from Paul and pray for the spiritual wellbeing of your brothers and sisters in Christ.

4 RAISED WITH CHRIST

The story so far

Christ's people are those who have been blessed by God with every spiritual blessing in Christ.

Christ's people have been saved by God—the Father, Son and Spirit—as part of God's great plan to bring everything in the universe under Christ's authority.

The people of Christ's new community have love for other Christians and, by the Spirit, grow in knowledge of God and understanding of their blessings.

⊕ talkabout

1. How do you view your past? Is it something you remember fondly? Something you want to forget? How relevant or irrelevant is it to who you are today?

⊕ investigate

▶ **Read Ephesians 2 v 1-3**

2. How does Paul describe the lives of these Ephesian Christians before they came to faith in Jesus (v 1)? What does Paul's choice of word here tell us about the condition of those who are still outside of Christ?

DICTIONARY

Transgressions (v 1): deliberate sins.
Ruler of the kingdom of the air (v 2): the devil.
Gratifying (v 3): satisfying.
Wrath (v 3): God's deserved anger and punishment.

3. This condition is caused by following what (v 2)? (Find two answers.)

4. Many try to blame their sin on the influence of the world or believe that "the devil made me do it". What's Paul's answer to this in verse 3?

5. In God's eyes, what is the status of those outside of Christ, and why (v 3)?

optional

⊡ explore more

> **Read Romans 1 v 18-32**

The Bible consistently links our wrongdoing with our rebellion against God.

What is mankind's attitude to God?
What behaviour results from this attitude?
What excuses for our behaviour are demolished in these verses (see v 20 and 32)?

Read the verdict of Scripture on human nature in **Romans 3 v 10-12**.

⇥ apply

The world's ideas about relationships, children, business, beauty, sex, etc. are all corrupt, and lead to death. Before we were Christians, we took on board the practices of the world with no suspicion, no resistance, no reflection, no thought for the fact that the end of the world's ways is death. We skipped merrily toward the deepest parts of hell.

6. Share examples of how this has been true in your life and what changed when you became a Christian.

⊥ **investigate**

"But ... God"! We should be so thankful for these two three-letter words that make all the difference in this world and the next.

▸ **Read Ephesians 2 v 4-10**

7. Find three words in verses 4-6 that sum up the character of God. What does each one mean for sinful people like us?

DICTIONARY
Mercy (v 4): not giving someone a punishment they deserve.

8. Why is it that people generally don't share this view of God's character? (Look at how verses 4-6 follow on from verses 1-3.)

9. Find the things that God has done in Christ for His people mentioned in the following verses:

• v 5:

• v 6:

• v 10:

10. What is God's ultimate purpose in our salvation (v 7)?

11. What is incompatible with God's grace (v 8-9)?

➔ apply

12. Ephesians 2 v 1-10 helps us understand what it is to be a true Christian. From these verses work out some of the characteristics that you would expect to find in a true Christian.

13. If you are a Christian, the love, mercy and grace of God has already come to you. The question is: how can you live more fully in recognition of His grace? Think about the difference God's grace to you will make in the following areas of your life:

• Your view of your sins:

• The way you treat others:

• Your part in the work God has given His people:

⊡ getting personal

Understanding the depth of our own personal sin and remembering daily how God has shown us rich mercy will lead us to confession, repentance, faith in Christ, gratitude to God, dependence on the Spirit and sacrificial commitment to our Saviour and Lord. What can you do to make sure that every day you remember and act on these truths?

⬆ pray

Together: Praise God for one aspect of His character and work that has particularly struck you in this session.

Alone: Make a list of things that you remember from your life before you came to faith in Jesus Christ—lying, selfishness, idolatry, promise-breaking... whatever gratifying the cravings of your sinful nature led to. Then remember the words of verse 4—"But ... God". Spend time talking to God about this.

5 Ephesians 2 v 11-22
UNITED IN CHRIST

The story so far

Christ's people have been saved by God—the Father, Son and Spirit—as part of God's great plan to bring everything in the universe under Christ's authority.

The people of Christ's new community have love for other Christians and, by the Spirit, grow in knowledge of God and understanding of their blessings.

We were once dead in sins, but God has now made us alive in Christ, raised us up with Christ, and given us good works to do for Him.

⊕ talkabout

1. Identify some groups in your community, area or nation that don't get on, and some of the conflicts that have resulted from these divisions. What solutions are often suggested and how successful are they?

⊕ investigate

❯ Read Ephesians 2 v 11-13

In 2 v 1-10, Paul has been calling the Ephesian Christians to remember what they once were before they were included in Christ. In verses 11-13, Paul repeats that basic message, but looks at how the gospel affects Jews and Gentiles in the church.

2. What words and phrases describe the status and experience of the Gentiles before they were included in Christ?

DICTIONARY

Gentiles (v 11): non-Jews.
"Uncircumcised" / "the circumcision" (v 12): in the Old Testament, circumcision was the physical sign of belonging to God's people (Genesis 17).
Covenants of the promise (v 12): God's promises to Abraham and his family.

3. How does Paul view those of Jewish birth? (What do you think is meant by his comment in verse 11 about "the circumcision"?)

4. What has now been done for these Gentiles, and how (v 13)?

▶ **Read Ephesians 2 v 14-22**

5. What is Paul emphasising in verse 14 when he says: "he himself"?

6. What four things has Jesus has done to bring us peace?
- v 14:

- v 14:

- v 15a:

- v 17:

⊡ **explore more**

optional

What importance is given to peace in the message of Jesus Christ?

▶ **Read Luke 2 v 8-14; 19 v 41-44; John 14 v 27; 16 v 33**

What do we learn here about the peace of the gospel?

⮕ apply

7. Based on what you have learned so far, how could you respond to people who say the following:

    a. *"We'll never have world peace until we all teach our children properly to respect and value all people equally."*

    b. *"Religion is what causes war, so Christianity can never be the answer to hatred and division."*

    c. *"I believe we have to find peace in our own hearts before we can expect to have world peace."*

⊡ getting personal

Are you lacking peace—in your relationships, in your own mind, and with God? Have you ever realised that maybe you lack peace because you are far from Jesus, even hostile to Him? It is through the preaching of the message of Jesus Christ that God intends you to discover His peace. How will you keep listening to God's message?

⬇ investigate

8. What did Jesus do in order to make peace (v 15b-16)?

9. Find two things that characterise Christ's new creation:

    • v 15:

    • v 16 and 18:

10. What three pictures illustrate Christ's community and our part in it?

    • v 19:

- v 19:

- v 22:

11. What do v 20-22 tell us about the foundation of Christ's new community?

⊡ **apply**

12. What difference does this passage make to your understanding of the Christian church?

13. In what practical ways will this teaching affect how you live, both individually and as a church?

⊡ **getting personal**

Does your allegiance to Christ come before all other allegiances? Do you describe yourself as an American/Korean/Nigerian/British Christian, or as a Christian American/Korean/Nigerian/British person? How can you show that you are first and foremost a citizen of God's kingdom and family in the way you live? Is there a particular racial or social group you feel distant from? How will you show your unity with Christians from that group?

↑ **pray**

Give thanks for Christ's new community—the church. Ask God to help you live out the truth of what Christ has done in your life.

6

Ephesians 3
GIVEN GOD'S MESSAGE

The story so far

The people of Christ's new community have love for other Christians and, by the Spirit, grow in knowledge of God and understanding of their blessings.

We were once dead in sins, but God has now made us alive in Christ, raised us up with Christ, and given us good works to do for Him.

Christ's new community comes from different nations, and has been reconciled to God through Christ. We are united into God's kingdom, family and temple.

⊕ talkabout

1. How do you feel about talking about the Christian faith with others? What do you struggle with? What gives you encouragement?

⊥ investigate

> ❯ Read Ephesians 3 v 1-13

2. Find three ways in which Paul describes himself as a messenger of God in these verses. What does each one tell us about this role?
   • v 1:

   • v 5 (also 1 v 1):

   • v 7:

DICTIONARY

Prisoner of Christ (v 1): Paul had been imprisoned for teaching about Jesus.
Administration (v 2, 9): giving.
Manifold (v 10): great and varied.
Rulers and authorities in the heavenly realms (v 10): powerful spiritual forces/beings.

3. How does Paul describe the gospel message in verse 3, and why (v 5)?

4. What is the "mystery" about (v 4-6)?

5. How do people come to understand the mystery of the gospel (v 4-5, 8-10)? Through whom and by which means?

6. The mystery of the gospel was something that even the greatest minds could not have discovered in Old Testament times. Why would this mystery (see v 6) be so surprising back then?

7. How does the mystery of the gospel—Christ's new community—become a reality (v 6)?

⊡ explore more

> **Read Matthew 28 v 18-20; Colossians 4 v 2-6; 1 Peter 3 v 15-16**

The apostle Paul carried out a unique task that was foundational to the church of Jesus Christ. We cannot take on that role because it has been completed.

optional

But what do these New Testament passages teach us about the role of all Christians in proclaiming the gospel?

→ apply

8. How does Paul's totally God-centred view of the gospel compare with the way the Christian faith is often understood and proclaimed today?

⊡ getting personal

The mysteries of God are not uncovered by human investigation, or research. They must be shown to us by God Himself. Any God we can comprehend through our own intellect is, by definition, an idol.

Have you been guilty of worshipping an idol of your own making? How can you start to seek and worship God as He truly is?

⊥ investigate

9. Why has God, through the gospel, created the church (v 10-11)?

▶ **Read Ephesians 3 v 14-21**

The profound significance of the church in God's eternal purpose, and the preciousness of these once-dead, once-excluded, once-estranged people for whom Christ has died, prompts Paul to pray for their spiritual wellbeing.

DICTIONARY
Established (v 17): firm, secure.
Surpasses (v 19): is greater than.
To the measure (v 19): full.

10. How do the following things feature in Paul's prayer for the Ephesians?

- strength:

- love:

- faith:

- understanding:

- knowledge:

- God the Father:

- Christ:

- the Holy Spirit:

- What do you imagine Christians would be like as a result of this prayer?

⮊ apply

11. Jesus has given to His church the task of proclaiming the gospel to all nations. From what you learned in this session, what is your part in that?

12. What have you learned about the importance of the church?

- What difference should that make in our discipleship and our outreach?

⬆ pray

"Now to him who is able to do immeasurably more than all we ask or imagine, according to his power that is at work within us…" Let this shape the confidence in which you now approach God in prayer.

7 Ephesians 4 v 1-16
GROWING IN CHRIST

The story so far

We were once dead in sins, but God has now made us alive in Christ, raised us up with Christ, and given us good works to do for Him.

Christ's new community comes from different nations, and has been reconciled to God through Christ. We are united into God's kingdom, family and temple.

God shows the universe His wisdom through the way His new community serves the gospel, worships together, and prays for each other.

⊕ talkabout

1. What advice would you give to someone who asks how they can grow as a Christian?

⬇ investigate

Here, Paul sets out the responsibilities that the people of Christ's new community have to one another, now that we have been united in Christ.

▶ Read Ephesians 4 v 1-6

2. Summarise our responsibility to one another, outlined in these verses.

> **DICTIONARY**
>
> **Calling (v 1):** God's command to follow Christ.
> **Bearing (v 2):** being patient

3. In light of the previous chapters, why do you think we are to do this?

4. What kind of people must we become (v 2)? Find three characteristics.

1.

2.

3.

- How will we think and act differently as we grow in each of these characteristics?

5. How are we to go about preserving unity? What do the following verses tell us?

- v 1:

- v 3:

- v 4-6:

⊖ apply

6. "To unite or not to unite?" What are the two opposing errors that Christians must guard against when confronted with this question?

• Which are you most prone to fall into? And how can you avoid it?

⊡ explore more

Chapter 4 focuses on the unity of the Spirit, and how Christians must make every effort to preserve it. But the New Testament also teaches that Christ's people must separate from false teachers.

*Read the following passages and note how we can identify those with whom we should not unite: **Matthew 7 v 15-23; Luke 6 v 26; Galatians 1 v 8-9; 1 Timothy 6 v 3-5; 1 John 2 v 18-19.***

⊡ getting personal

How are you doing with being humble, gentle and patient? Do you always consider the needs of others before your own? Do you realise that it's better to suffer wrong from others than to commit wrong against them or fail to forgive them? Do you understand that our only "entitlement" is the wrath of God in hell because of our sins? Do you live in the Bible's teaching that "God opposes the proud but shows grace to the humble" (James 4 v 6)?

⊡ investigate

> ▶ **Read Ephesians 4 v 7-16**

7. What responsibility to each other does Paul highlight in these verses (v 12-13; also v 16)?

> **DICTIONARY**
>
> **Apportioned (v 7):** gave.
> **The body of Christ (v 12):** the church, ie: Christians.

8.   What goal is in view here (v 13-16)?

• How will we know that the goal is being achieved (v 14-15)?

9.   What has Christ given to the church to bring this about (v 11)?

• What grounds do we have to be confident about how the church has been equipped (v 7-10)?

10.   How do Christ's people become servants (v 11-12a)?

➔ apply

11. In light of what you have learned in this session, would you adjust your advice to the Christian who wants to grow in faith (Question 1)? How?

• How should we apply this to ourselves?

12. What will it mean for us to speak the truth in love (v 15)?

⊡ getting personal

What are you doing to serve your Christian brothers and sisters in the church and build them up? What are you doing to make sure that you are prepared and equipped for that service? What's your role in keeping the unity of the Spirit in your church?
Think and pray about changes you may need to make in order to get involved with God's people as He intends you to be.

⬆ pray

Together: Praise God for the gifts that Christ has given to your church to grow His people in unity and maturity. Pray that your Christian fellowship will keep united in the Spirit and growing in faith and knowledge of Jesus Christ.

Alone: Ask God to help you with what has especially challenged you in this session—in particular, your role in your local church.

8
Ephesians 4 v 17 – 5 v 17
CLOTHED WITH NEW LIFE

The story so far

Christ's new community comes from different nations, and has been reconciled to God through Christ. We are united into God's kingdom, family and temple.

God shows the universe His wisdom through the way His new community serves the gospel, worships together, and prays for each other.

The people of Christ's new community are given gifts by Him to be used to serve the church, so that it can grow in unity and faith.

⊕ talkabout

1. How do people change when they come to faith in Jesus Christ?

⊕ investigate

▶ **Read Ephesians 4 v 17-24**

2. What does Paul insist on here (v 17)?

3. How do the Gentiles live (v 17-19)? What is said about...
- their minds?

- their spiritual condition?

- their consciences?

- their behaviour?

4. Why do they live this way (v 18)?

5. What is the only alternative to the Gentiles' way of life (v 20-21)?

6. How did the Ephesians change from one way of life to the other? Find four things that they were taught.
- v 21:

- v 22:

- v 23:

- v 24:

➔ apply

7. What's the relationship between faith (the Christian's response to the truth that is in Jesus) and action (the Christian's response to teaching about putting off the old self and putting on the new self)?

• What is God's part and what is our part?

8. What should we expect a good church to teach?

• We've seen that Christians need to be taught how to put off the old self and put on the new self. How should the importance of this teaching affect our involvement in our church?

⊕ investigate

▶ Read Ephesians 4 v 25-32

9. How will we look in our "new clothes"? For instance...
• How will we / how won't we speak (v 25, 29)?

• What will we do, and not do, with our hands (v 28)?

• How will we, and how won't we, respond in our hearts when something makes us angry (v 26-27, 31-32)?

10. Who is affected by our failure or refusal to put on our new clothes (v 30)?

⊡ **explore more**

optional

▶ **Read Ephesians 5 v 1-17**

In these verses Paul continues to rub in the themes of his letter so far—the dramatic turnaround in the life of a believer, the old clothes that we must put off and the new clothes we need to put on.

What old clothes and new clothes does Paul add here?
How does he sum up our new life in Christ (v 2, 8, 15)? And the old life (v 5, 6, 15 and 17)?
What reasons does he give that should motivate us to live out our new life in Christ (v 2, 5-6, 16)?
What action do we need to take (v 1, 6, 10, 16, 17)?

→ **apply**

11. What would most encourage you to put on the new self?

• What can you do to encourage the same in others?

⊡ getting personal

How forgiving are you? God has forgiven you at the expense of His only Son—so can you honestly withhold forgiveness from anyone? Can you justify before Jesus your anger, bitterness, malice, rage, anger or slander? Can you look at the one who was despised, rejected, spat upon, mocked and beaten... and say: "I'm justified in treating others the way you were treated for me"?

It's better to be defrauded than be like 4 v 31. It's better to taste something of the Saviour's suffering than turn away from a brother with unforgiveness in our hearts.

⊕ pray

"Put on the new self, created to be like God in true righteousness and holiness." Praise God for the "new you" that He has created. Thank Him for His word, His Holy Spirit and the people in your church—used by Him to change you.

Confess and repent of old clothes which you have not yet put off. Pray about areas of your life that still need changing in order for you to be more like Christ.

9 Ephesians 5 v 18 – 6 v 9
FILLED WITH THE SPIRIT

The story so far

God shows the universe His wisdom through the way His new community serves the gospel, worships together, and prays for each other.

The people of Christ's new community are given gifts by Him to be used to serve the church, so that it can grow in unity and faith.

We have our minds renewed through the teaching of the truth about Jesus, so we can put off our old sinful selves and put on our new, holy, righteous selves.

⊕ talkabout

1. How do you feel about authority? What do you think when you hear the word "authority"?

⊕ investigate

> Read Ephesians 5 v 18-21

2. What is prohibited in verse 18? And what is commanded?

DICTIONARY
Debauchery (v 18): sexual sin.
Submit to (v 21): follow the lead of/ accept the authority of.
Reverence (v 21): deep respect.

3. Paul deliberately contrasts being drunk with being filled with the Holy Spirit. What one effect on people do they have in common?

4. What does drunkenness lead to?

5. What does being filled with the Spirit lead to?

6. Look at the characteristics of a Spirit-filled person. What does each mean in practice?

• v 19a:

• v 19b:

• v 20:

• v 21:

7. What's the connection in these verses between the Spirit and Christ?

⤷ apply

8. How is Paul's description of a Spirit-filled person different from what you expected, or from other ideas you have heard about being Spirit-filled?

• How can we know if someone is a Spirit-filled person?

⊡ getting personal

Are you sometimes attracted to a way of life where the greatest thrill on offer is the "freedom" of drunkenness? This world's idea of the good life is utterly paltry when compared to the Spirit-filled life. Why give up control of your mind to that which can only bring shame, waste, regret and harm, when you could have the transformed, abundant life that comes from a mind controlled by the third Person of the Trinity?

⊡ explore more

optional

There is lots of confusion about the work of the Spirit, leading to questions like: "Who has the Spirit?" "When does a Christian receive the Spirit?" and "Do all Christians have the Spirit or only some?"

▶ Read Titus 3 v 4-7; Ephesians 1 v 13-14

How does the New Testament answer these questions?

▶ Read Galatians 5 v 25; Ephesians 4 v 30

Do all Christians benefit equally from the Spirit?
Where does Paul's command to be filled with the Spirit fit in?

⬇ investigate

❯ Read Ephesians 5 v 22 – 6 v 9

Paul focuses on three areas of life—marriage, parenting and work—to show us what godly submission and authority look like in everyday life.

DICTIONARY

Radiant (v 27): shining, beautiful.
Profound (v 32): very great.

9. Fill in the table. Notice how Paul links behaviour with truth about Christ.

Verses	Who?	What's the command?	How? (link with Christ)	Why?
5 v 22-24				
5 v 25-32				
6 v 1-3				
6 v 4				
6 v 5-8				
6 v 9				

⊡ apply

10. What does marriage in particular show us about Christ and how should this affect the way that wives and husbands relate to each other?

11. What does Paul's teaching here mean for…
• children?

• fathers?

12. What does Paul's teaching here mean for…
• workers?

• bosses?

⊡ getting personal

Christian marriages picture Jesus and the church; a child's obedience shows that God's ways are best; a worker's obedience demonstrates that God is the greatest Rewarder of people. What does your life say about God? How is the truth about Jesus seen clearly in the way you live?

⬆ pray

Together: Start today a habit of giving God thanks for everything—especially for the way in which Christ loves the church and has given Himself up for us.

Alone: Ask God to help you change in one area of your life about which you have been especially challenged in this session.

Ephesians 6 v 10-24
O READY FOR BATTLE

The story so far

The people of Christ's new community are given gifts by Him to be used to serve the church, so that it can grow in unity and faith.

We have our minds renewed through the teaching of the truth about Jesus, so we can put off our old sinful selves and put on our new, holy, righteous selves.

The Spirit directs our minds and transforms our behaviour, so that we display God's grace and love in our everyday actions and relationships.

⊕ talkabout

1. What do you think is the main reason why many Christians pray so little and so rarely?

⊥ investigate

> ❯ Read Ephesians 6 v 10-18

2. Summarise the situation that the church faces in this world. What does this mean for our Christian lives?

3. What do we learn about our opponent (v 11-12)?

4. Where does strength for this battle come from, and how do we get this for ourselves (v 10-11)?

5. What can we then do against this opponent (v 11, 13, 14)?

• Why do you think we are commanded to do only this and not more?

⊡ apply

6. Look at Paul's description of the Christian's spiritual armour (v 14-17). For each piece, what does it mean in practice to put it on? And what would it look like if you neglected to put it on?

• The belt of truth (v 14):

• The breastplate of righteousness (v 14):

• The shoes (ESV) of the gospel of peace (v 15):

• The shield of faith (v 16):

• The helmet of salvation (v 17):

• The sword of the Spirit (v 17):

explore more

> **Read Isaiah 11 v 5; 52 v 7; 59 v 17**

What are the parallels with the description of the armour of God in Ephesians 6?

God is, in fact, a Warrior for His people. The armour we are to wear is the armour that "the Redeemer" (59 v 20) wears as He comes to rescue God's people. It is the armour Christ has already worn in saving us from sin, death, hell and the judgment of God.

⬇ investigate

7. In verse 18 what do we learn about the final piece of God's armour—prayer.

• How are we to pray?

• When?

• What kinds of prayers are mentioned?

• Who for?

> **Read Ephesians 6 v 19-24**

DICTIONARY

Ambassador (v 20): representative.

8. What do we learn about the quality of relationships between those mentioned in these closing verses? And what is done to maintain those relationships?

9. Look at Paul's personal prayer request (v 19-20). How does it compare with what you might ask people to pray for you in Paul's situation?

⮕ apply

10. What could you do to bring your prayers—both alone and together with other Christians—in line with Paul's teaching and example here?

☺ getting personal

Do you have set times of private prayer scheduled into your day and week? How often and how regularly do you meet with other Christians in your church specifically to pray? If prayer is something that you have neglected, what does that say about your state of readiness for the struggle against God's enemy? You can only be strong *"in the Lord* and *in his mighty power"*.

11. What could you do to strengthen your relationships with fellow Christians, both in your local church and beyond?

⬆ pray

"Finally, be strong in the Lord and in his mighty power."

Praise God that Christ has already defeated sin, death, and the devil. Thank God for all the privileges and blessings of Christ's people that you have learned about in Ephesians.

Pray that by the power of the Spirit you and your Christian brothers and sisters will continue in Christ to the glory of God the Father.

God's big plan for Christ's new people
LEADER'S GUIDE

Leader's Guide

INTRODUCTION

Leading a Bible study can be a bit like herding cats—everyone has a different idea of what the passage could be about, and a different line of enquiry that they want to pursue. But a good group leader is more than someone who just referees this kind of discussion. You will want to:

- correctly understand and handle the Bible passage. But also...

- encourage and train the people in your group to do this for themselves. Don't fall into the trap of spoon-feeding people by simply passing on the information in the Leader's Guide. Then...

- make sure that no Bible study is finished without everyone knowing how the passage is relevant for them. What changes do you all need to make in the light of the things you have been learning? And finally...

- encourage the group to turn all that has been learned and discussed into prayer.

Your Bible-study group is unique, and you are likely to know better than anyone the capabilities, backgrounds and circumstances of the people you are leading. That's why we've designed these guides with a number of optional features. If they're a quiet bunch, you might want to spend longer on *talkabout*. If your time is limited, you can choose to skip *explore more*, or get people to look at these questions at home. Can't get enough of Bible study? Well, some studies have optional extra homework projects. As leader, you can adapt and select the material to the needs of your particular group.

So what's in the Leader's Guide? The main thing that this Leader's Guide will help you to do is to understand the major teaching points in the passage you are studying, and how to apply them. As well as guidance on the questions, the Leader's Guide for each session contains the following important sections:

THE BIG IDEA

One or two key sentences will give you the main point of the session. This is what you should be aiming to have fixed in people's minds as they leave the Bible study. And it's the point you need to head back toward when the discussion goes off at a tangent.

SUMMARY

An overview of the passage, including plenty of useful historical background information.

OPTIONAL EXTRA

Usually this is an introductory activity that ties in with the main theme of the Bible study, and is designed to "break the ice" at the beginning of a session. Or it may be a "homework project" that people can tackle during the week.

So let's take a look at the various different features of a Good Book Guide:

⊕ talkabout

Each session kicks off with a discussion question, based on the group's opinions or experiences. It's designed to get people talking and thinking in a general way about the main subject of the Bible study.

⊥ investigate

The first thing you and your group need to know is what the Bible passage is about, which is the purpose of these questions. But watch out—people may come up with answers based on their experiences or teaching they have heard in the past, without referring to the passage at all. It's amazing how often we can get through a Bible study without actually looking at the Bible! If you're stuck for an answer, the Leader's Guide contains guidance for questions. These are the answers to direct your group to. This information isn't meant to be read out to people—ideally, you want them to discover these answers from the Bible for themselves. Sometimes there are optional follow-up questions (see ☑ in guidance on questions) to help you help your group get to the answer.

⊡ explore more

These questions generally point people to other relevant parts of the Bible. They are useful for helping your group to see how the passage fits into the "big picture" of the whole Bible. These sections are OPTIONAL—only use them if you have time. Remember that it's better to finish in good time having really grasped one big thing from the passage, than to try and cram everything in.

⤷ apply

We want to encourage you to spend more time working at application—too often, it is simply tacked on at the end. In the Good Book Guides, apply sections are mixed in with the investigate sections of the study. We hope that people will realize that application is not just an optional extra, but rather, the whole purpose of studying the

Bible. We do Bible study so that our lives can be changed by what we hear from God's word. If you skip the application, the Bible study hasn't achieved its purpose.

These questions draw out practical lessons that we can all learn from the Bible passage. You can review what has been learned so far, and think about practical differences that this should make in our churches and our lives. The group gets the opportunity to talk about what they personally have learned.

⊡ getting personal

These can be done at home, but it is well worth allowing a few moments of quiet reflection during the study for each person to think and pray about specific changes they need to make in their own lives. Why not have a time for reporting back at the beginning of the following session, so that everyone can be encouraged and challenged by one another to make application a priority?

⊤ pray

In Acts 4 v 25-30 the first Christians quoted Psalm 2 as they prayed in response to the persecution of the apostles by the Jewish religious leaders. Today however, it's not as common for Christians to base prayers on the truths of God's word as it once was. As a result, our prayers tend to be weak, superficial and self-centred rather than bold, visionary and God-centred.

The prayer section is based on what has been learned from the Bible passage. How different our prayer times would be if we were genuinely responding to what God has said to us through His word.

1 Ephesians 1 v 1-14
BLESSED IN CHRIST

THE BIG IDEA
Christ's people are those who have been blessed by God with every spiritual blessing in Christ.

SUMMARY
Ephesians gives us perhaps the clearest statement on what church really is and the eternal plan of God for His people. God has purposed that there will be a collection, an assembly, a corporate body of His people—called the "church". And amazingly, Ephesians tells us that the church—the Christian community and not "lone ranger" Christians—stands at the centre of God's plan for both heaven and earth.

We begin by looking at the gripping story of how the Ephesian church came into being, told in Acts 19—dramatic events that were later reflected in some of the themes of Paul's letter. Clearly, Paul doesn't write to the Ephesians from some ivory tower; nor are his instructions to them nice but unrealistic ideas that can never be put into practice. He writes out of his experience in Ephesus, having seen God at work in the lives of the Ephesian believers, transforming both obstinate followers of Judaism, and ignorant pagans into a new, united body of those who are growing more like Christ.

In this first session we learn that:
1. The world is divided into two groups of people—those who are "in Christ" and all others who are outside of Christ.
2. Christians—those in Christ—have received every spiritual blessing in Him, meaning that there is *nothing* that we need to live and keep going as believers that God has not provided us with in His Son. (This session introduces the blessings from God that Paul has listed in verses 4-14, but these verses are not investigated in detail until next session.)

The main challenge of this session is to believe, if we are Christians, that we have received every spiritual blessing in Christ and to live in the light of that, especially in tough times when we are tempted to think that the Christian life is too difficult.

OPTIONAL EXTRA
This starter activity is designed both to break the ice in your group (if needed) and to introduce the theme of the whole book of Ephesians that is highlighted in this Good Book Guide. It therefore overlaps with question 1 (talkabout).

Go through a list of words/phrases that people commonly use to describe their view of "church". Don't mention "church"—see how long it takes your group to guess the subject of these words/phrases. Make sure you leave the more obvious ones for later. For instance, a new Christian, recalling his response to church as a non-Christian, summed it up with the word "grey"! You could start with something like this and then add words such as: weird, uncomfortable, boring, effeminate (whatever suits your group), before mentioning the more recognisable comments such as: "full of hypocrites", "only for losers", or "only after your money". Google something like "quotations about church", select some of the more cynical views and find out whether people once thought in the same way about church (or perhaps still do!). Finally, encourage your group to look out for God's very different view of His church in this session and throughout Ephesians.

GUIDANCE ON QUESTIONS

1. What words or phrases come to mind when you think of the word "church"?
Depending on your group, you can either focus on the more common reactions of both non-Christians and poorly taught or disaffected Christians, or you could use this question as an opportunity to review what Bible teaching about church your group knows, and examine how much that matches or differs from people's personal views of church.

- **To what extent do you relate to these views of "church"?**

Note: You should aim to proceed fairly quickly through Q2–7.

2. Who did Paul preach to in Ephesus (v 8-10)? He preached first to the Jews in the synagogue, then to the Gentiles in a discussion hall, so that all the Jews and Gentiles in the province of Asia heard the word of the Lord (v 10). A whole section of Paul's letter is devoted to the power of the gospel to unite Jews and Gentiles into one body of people (see Session 5).

3. Contrast the message that Paul brought to Ephesus with the beliefs already held by some there (v 1-6). What happened to those who accepted the message preached by Paul? Among the Jews in Ephesus there were disciples of John the Baptist, who had not heard about Jesus—the one to whom John himself pointed. When they did hear about Christ, the Holy Spirit came on them just as He

had come to the first believers at Pentecost. In his letter Paul speaks of both the pre-eminence of Christ and of the work of the Spirit in the lives of those who are included in Christ (see Session 3).

- **How did people change when they accepted this message (v 17-20)?** The influence of the Spirit in the lives of these new Christians can be seen in the way that new Christians openly confessed their former evil deeds. Some even destroyed belongings associated with their previous way of life. They understood that they needed to cut themselves off from their old ways, a theme that takes up a major part of Ephesians (see Sessions 4, 8 and 9).

4. What other responses were there (v 9, 13)? Some of the Jews refused to believe (v 9). This was nothing to do with Paul's lack of communication skills or any irrationality in what he said—he argued "boldly" and "persuasively". It was because they were "obstinate" and "refused to believe". As Paul later puts it in his letter, they were controlled by "the spirit who is now at work in those who are disobedient" (Ephesians 2 v 2). Some of the Jews tried to win prestige and personal gain by using the name of the Lord Jesus in an (unsuccessful) attempt to exorcise evil spirits (v 13). These unbelievers illustrate what Paul means when he describes people in their sins as following the desires and thoughts of their sinful natures, and as objects of God's wrath (Ephesians 2 v 1-3).

5. What was the reason for Demetrius' opposition (v 25-27), and what does this tell us about the new Ephesian Christians? The first reason was economic—he feared loss of income in his business of manufacturing silver shrines of Artemis. The second was a religious reason—he feared that the religion of Artemis would suffer a great loss of prestige. All this shows the depth of radical transformation in the people who had turned to Christ. There was no question of simply adding Jesus to the religion they had been brought up in, nor of secretly following Christ while continuing in their old ways. These first Ephesian Christians understood that they "must no longer live as the Gentiles do" (Ephesians 4 v 17), and the effect of their transformation was immediate and far-reaching. The change could not be ignored, resulting in hostility and violence from their opponents. The church in Ephesus was born into a state of spiritual warfare (see Ephesians 6 v 10-13).

6. What was the city clerk's verdict on Paul and his colleagues (v 37)? The city clerk was clearly a pagan, not a Christian. However, he concluded that Paul and his colleagues had done nothing wrong. They could not be blamed in any way for the commotion. Rather, it was caused by the darkened minds and hardened hearts of the Gentile pagans, enslaved to their passions and lusts. Again we can see the stark difference between the old, sinful way of life, and the new life of righteousness, created in those who are included in Christ.

7. Paul spent three years in Ephesus (v 31). What does verse 17 show had resulted from his time there? Paul left behind him a church, with elders who would continue in the task of leading Christ's people in Ephesus, after Paul had moved on. The preciousness of this church to Paul becomes evident in this letter (eg: 1 v 15-19a; 3 v 14-19), and the place of the church in the purposes of God is one of the great themes of the book of Ephesians. **Note:** You could split this study here!

8. [In Ephesians 1 v 1-3] Who is this letter from, how is he described, and who is it addressed to? *From:* Paul (v 1). *Description:* "an apostle" or messenger. Specifically, he is a messenger "of Christ Jesus by the will of God." That is, he is not a carrier of his own ideas or words, but he carries the ideas and thoughts of Jesus Christ, according to the wishes of God. *To:* Paul writes this letter to "God's holy people ["saints", NIV84] ... the faithful in Christ Jesus" in the city of Ephesus. "Holy people/saints" means "sanctified ones," people "set apart" or "cleansed". This refers to any and all Christians. It's not a special title given to certain special Christians, but describes all those who are "faithful in Christ Jesus" (v 1)—that is, all who trust in Jesus and have therefore been "set apart" for His use, and to worship Him.

• **How should this shape our attitude to these studies?** All that was true then for these original recipients is true now for us. We are recipients of a letter from God Himself by a messenger sent by the will of God. The following questions are a checklist that your group might find helpful in ascertaining how well they are paying attention.

9. What exactly does verse 3 tell us about the blessings that Christians receive from God? (When, where, how much and how?) Notice how sweeping the statement in verse 3 is. When? God "has blessed us"—it's already done. Where? "in the heavenly realms"—our new residence, God's unshakeable kingdom of absolute security, where nothing can get lost, stolen or damaged (Hebrews 12 v 27-28; Matthew 6 v 19-20). How much? "with every spiritual blessing"—nothing has been left out or forgotten. How? "in Christ"—He is the source of all spiritual blessing; none of this is available to us if we are not in a right relationship with Him.

10. What does "every spiritual blessing" look like? To help you answer this question, fill in the table... See table below/over the page. These spiritual blessings will be examined in much greater detail in the next session, so don't let your group worry if/when they do not fully understand each verse. Column Four should be left to be filled in after Q6 in Study Two.

☑

(Ask after table has been filled in.)

• **Pick out one aspect of what you've seen that you understand, and that you find exciting or encouraging.**

11. In the first 14 verses of Ephesians, how many times is the phrase "in Christ" (including "in him" and "in the One he loves") used? Ten times (v 1, 3, 4, 6, 7, 9, 11, 12, 13 (twice); plus a reference to "redemption through his blood" (v 7).

• **What truth does this emphasise?** These blessings are *only* found in Christ, in relationship with Him. Jesus is essential to all of the Father's work in redeeming sinners—so central that only in Him are we saved from God's wrath, and only in

Verses	What is the blessing from God?	What else is said about this blessing?	What difference does it make? (Study Two)
v 4	He chose us	1. *Who?* Those in Christ 2. *When?* Before the creation of the world 3. *For what?* To be holy and blameless	1. Our status as a Christian doesn't depend on our effort or choice. 2. We should live for hte purpose for which we've been chosen.
v 5	He predestined us to be adopted as His Sons	1. *How?* Through Jesus Christ 2. *Why did God do this?* Because He wanted to	Whatever our worldly status, we have the incredible privilege of being a child of God
v 6	He has freely given us "grace" (= undeserved	*How?* Through Jesus Christ	We don't deserve anything from God. Whatever we've done, He shows Christians kindness
v 7	He has "redeemed" us (=paid the price necessary to buy us out of slavery)	1. *How?* Through the blood of Christ 2. *What does that mean for us?* Forgiveness of sins.	We are free to fight against sin, and free from the fear of death (see Romans 6 v 6-14). We can revel in being forgiven by God
v 8	He has given us all wisdom and understanding		We can understand all sorts of things that non-Christians cannot (eg: Eph 1 v 17-22)

Verses	What is the blessing from God?	What else is said about this blessing?	What difference does it make? (Study Two)
v 9-10	He has made known to us the mystery of His will	*What is His will?* To bring everything under Christ at the end of history	We know where the history of the universe is heading, and we can make sure our lives reflect God's purposes. Whatever the future holds, we know it ends with our blessed Saviour
v 11	He has given us an inheritance. *"We were also chosen" (NIV) is better translated as "we have obtained an inheritance" (ESV)*		We are heirs of God and co-heirs with Christ (Romans 8 v 17) and we can look forward to riches in heaven beyond imagination (see 1 Peter 1 v 4)
v 13a	He has included us in Christ	*When?* When we heard and believed the gospel	Our lives are blended together with Jesus (see Explore More below)
v 13-14	He has sealed us with the Holy Spirit	*What does the Holy Spirit do for us?* He helps us to enjoy a foretaste now of what we will enjoy in eternity	We can eagerly and patiently look forward to eternity (Romans 8 v 22-25)

Him can we obtain spiritual blessing and an inheritance. This emphasises that the whole world is divided into two groups—in Christ or outside of Christ. People who are not yet Christians have not yet received "every spiritual blessing". Some people experience *every* spiritual blessing: the rest experience *none*. The love of God is not an automatic right. God is in control of His affections infinitely more than we are in control of ours. If it's right that we should choose whom we give our love to, how much more is it good and right that God should do so? He chooses to place His special, saving love only on His people—those "in Christ".

EXPLORE MORE
Read Ephesians 1 v 13; 2 Corinthians 5 v 21; Galatians 2 v 20. What details do we find here about what it means to be "in Christ"?

Ephesians 1 v 13: To be "included in Christ" happens when we hear and believe the gospel. It means to become a Christian.

2 Corinthians 5 v 21: In Christ we become "the righteousness of God". In other words, God's holy requirement that we are perfect as He is perfect (Matthew 5 v 48) is met by Christians being united with Jesus Christ. Any righteousness of ours is like filthy rags (Isaiah 64 v 6), but God sees Christ's righteousness in us instead. Our unity with

Christ completely changes our legal status before God.

Galatians 2 v 20: The Christian can say that "I no longer live, but Christ lives in me". A glance at verse 19 helps us to understand what this means—the Christian is finished with the old way of life of a lawbreaker, and because of being united with Christ is now able to live for God. We continue to live in the same old body, but now we operate our lives according to "faith in the Son of God". Our unity with Christ completely changes the way we live our lives.

Read 1 Cor 6 v 14-20; 2 Cor 6 v 14-17. What does this mean for us in practice?
It's our union with Christ that prompts Paul to instruct Christians to avoid sexual immorality. He underlines that if a Christian goes with a prostitute it means joining Christ with a prostitute. What we do with our bodies, we also do with Jesus' body (1 Corinthians 6 v 14-20). And it's union with Christ that causes Paul to tell Christians not to be unequally yoked with non-believers eg: not to marry non-Christians (2 Corinthians 6 v 14-17). This teaching—

that we are united together with Jesus—is meant to touch and purify every area of our lives. The practical principle is this: If it would be inappropriate or wrong for Jesus to do or be joined with such a thing, then we should not do it or join with it because we are united with Christ through faith in Him.

12. APPLY: What troubles you at the moment—tempting you to question whether you can go on as a Christian?
Be sensitive to the fact that people in your group may not yet be ready to share their personal struggles. As an alternative, ask: "What kinds of situations are most likely to make you question whether you can go on as a Christian?"

• **How does v 3 help us in these troubles, temptations and questions?**
Whatever we think we lack in order to live the Christian life, whatever spiritual quality or ability we think we are missing in order to be Christ-like, it is already provided to us in Christ! If we think we lack anything, we are wrong!

2 Ephesians 1 v 3-14
SAVED BY GOD

THE BIG IDEA
Christ's people have been saved by the concerted activity of God in the persons of the Father, Son and Spirit, in accordance with God's great plan of bringing everything in the universe under the headship of Christ.

SUMMARY
Last session we saw that Christ's people have received every spiritual blessing in Christ; in this session we look in greater

detail at what having "every spiritual blessing" looks like. We see what the business world might label an "acquisitions team"—God the Father, the Son and the Holy Spirit, who work together to acquire souls for the church and for God's glory.

We learn that:

1. God has done everything needed for us to be saved and become His people. There is no place in this for anything we do, or any merit on our part.

2. The Father, Son and Holy Spirit all work together in different roles with the same purpose—to bring glory to God by saving sinners and bringing them into the church as part of God's great plan of bringing everything in the universe under the headship of Christ.

This session introduces people to some major doctrines—election and predestination, adoption and redemption, the indwelling of the Spirit, the perseverance of the saints and God's purpose for all of creation and history. There are many practical implications and applications that you could spend time on, but this session focuses on the grounds for our assurance as Christians; the link between understanding the gospel and praising God; and how understanding God's purpose in creation and history will shape our priorities and those of our church.

OPTIONAL EXTRA

Imagine someone outside the church asks: "What does a Christian mean when they say that they are 'saved'?" Get your group to share what they might say in answer to this, and write up the key words on a whiteboard/flipchart. You could return to your list at the end of the session and see how similar/different it is to Paul's great description in Ephesians 1 v 4-14.

GUIDANCE ON QUESTIONS

1. How confident are you that you are forgiven by God and that you will be saved from condemnation on the Day of Judgment? Do you change from day to day? If so, what increases your confidence, and what makes you sometimes doubt your salvation? Most Christians will admit to wavering from time to time on this issue, and some may have very deep and bitter struggles (and may need further help outside the session). Lack of assurance is usually linked with how well or badly Christians judge they have lived up to God's standards. This shows how we are deeply prone to lapsing into relying on our own good works to save us, and underlines the importance of constantly reminding ourselves that salvation is all of God's grace and none of our merit. The truths covered in this session are just such a reminder.

2. ... What does each member of the Trinity specifically do in this work of saving us to become part of God's people?

- **The Father (v 4-6):** The key words are "chose", "predestined" and "adoption". The Father chose us and predestined us to become saints, before the creation of the world. Aeons before we were born, conceived or imagined—before we could do or think anything—God chose His people for Himself. This is known as "election", and, despite the clear teaching of the Bible (as here), it is controversial for some Christians.

  It may be helpful to show your group that Jesus taught the same thing. Eg: In John 17 v 2 He talks about giving eternal life to all the Father has given to Him. In eternity past the Father promised to give to the Son a people for His own, and Ephesians 1 v 4 tells us that the process of doing so began with God choosing some to be holy and blameless. The Bible's teaching on election is investigated further in Q3.

- **The Son (v 7-12):** The key words are "redemption", "blood" and "forgiveness". Our redemption and the forgiveness of our sins are through Christ's blood. The Son of God entered space and time to redeem the people of God with His blood and to unite them to Himself. It is through His bloody death on the cross that the grace of God is seen. The Son has redeemed us from our sin and the wrath of God on the Day of Judgment by dying as our substitute—taking upon Himself the punishment we deserve.

- **The Holy Spirit (v 13-14):** The key words are "seal" and "deposit". God the Holy Spirit seals and keeps the Christian safe until eternity comes. There is far more the Holy Spirit does, but nothing more important than marking us out as belonging to God by giving us ears to hear the gospel and the gift of faith (see 1 Corinthians 2 v 12-14), and then preserving us (helping us to keep going) until the final redemption.

3. What is God's choice based on (v 4, 5, 11)? His love (v 4; see also 2 Thessalonians 2 v 13). In addition, verses 5 and 11 tell us that God chooses and predestines His saints "in accordance with his pleasure and will" and "according to [his] plan". He does it because it pleases Him to do so. No one coerces Him, suggests it to Him or tricks Him. God is sovereign in His choice to save. Note: If people in your group are struggling to reconcile God's fairness and His election, it may be worth spending extra time on this issue after the Bible study or in a separate session. For a brief yet biblical summary, see the chapter entitled "Election" in *Bitesize Theology* by Peter Jeffrey, published by Evangelical Press. Or refer to a good systematic theology eg: Chapter 32 of *Systematic Theology* by Wayne Grudem, published by Zondervan (US)/IVP (UK).

4. What does the word "adoption" (v 5) tell us about the change from our old way of life as unbelievers to our new life in Christ? Before the world began, God decided to adopt each Christian as His own child. Before God acted to include us in Christ, we were not one of His children,

even though many people assume they are on account of God being their Creator (see, for example, John 8 v 39-47). When we are included in Christ we can, for the first time, approach God as our Father.

⌄

- **What difference should our adoption by God make in our everyday lives (Romans 8 v 15-17; Matthew 7 v 9-11)?** As God's children we are no longer afraid of Him. Instead we have a relationship of intimacy and dependence on Him—we call Him Abba—a child's term for their father. We have become an heir of God (compare Ephesians 1 v 14). In Matthew 7, Jesus assures us that our Father in heaven gives good gifts to those who ask Him. To summarise, being adopted by God should affect how and why we pray to Him, and give us hope and confidence for the future, as we look forward to our inheritance.

5. "Redemption" means being purchased out of slavery. What does this tell us about how our life changes when we are included in Christ? God has paid a price to purchase us out of slavery to sin, death, Satan and judgment, and to bring us back to Himself. There is nothing that anyone can do to escape this slavery, but the price has been paid by the blood of Jesus.

⌄

- **How should our redemption and forgiveness affect our everyday lives (1 Peter 1 v 18 – 2 v 1)?** We should no longer live the empty way of life handed down from our forefathers. We can now live a life of faith and hope in God, love for one another, and ridding ourselves of sin. 1 John tells us that when we do sin, we can be confident of God's forgiveness through Christ. We are no longer burdened by guilt and condemnation.

6. A better translation of "we were also chosen" (v 11) is "we have obtained an inheritance" (ESV). What does this tell us, first about our life in this world and then our life in the future? Christians do not experience "every blessing" in this world. Verse 3 tells us that God has blessed us "in the heavenly realms", and v 14 talks of the Spirit guaranteeing our inheritance until a point in the future when God will fully redeem His people (compare Romans 8 v 18-25). The apostle Peter says we have "an inheritance that can never perish, spoil or fade. This inheritance is kept in heaven for you" (1 Peter 1 v 4). Blessed as we are now, we still struggle with sin, sickness, suffering, disappointment, persecution, and decaying bodies. But we are spiritually rich in heaven beyond imagination! Our life in eternity with Christ will be incomparably better, and it is this guaranteed hope that keeps us going in tough times. See 2 Cor 4 v 16-17.

EXPLORE MORE
Read Romans 8 v 5-28. List the characteristics of someone who has the Spirit. They set their minds on what the Spirit desires (v 5) and submit to God's law (v 7); are confident of resurrection despite their failing bodies, and look forward to it patiently (v 11, 23); fight strenuously against sin in their own bodies (v 13); no longer fear God but are confident that He accepts them as His children (v 15-16); pray to God in the assurance that the Spirit will intercede for them even when they do not know how to pray (v 26-27); know that God works for our good and according to His purpose in whatever situation comes our way (v 28).

Note: At this point you should return to the table in Study One (p10-11) and complete the fourth column together. (Suggested answers on p65-66.)

7. APPLY: How can we know for certain if we have been saved or not? How might this Bible passage help you to help someone who is unsure that they are truly saved? Notice what is absent in these verses: our good deeds; baptism, communion or any other rite; church membership, styles of dress or hair etc. In other words, what is missing is anything that we do. If we struggle—as many Christians do—with whether or not we are saved, we need to think and pray about whether our certainty about being saved rests on the wrong grounds. Our salvation does not depend on us and neither does our preservation as one of Christ's people. The God who chose us before the creation of the world... the Son who has redeemed us with His own blood... and the Holy Spirit who seals us until final redemption... cannot fail to keep us safe on that terrible Day of Judgment, and until then. Make sure all of your hope rests on what God has done to save you, and make these the grounds for your assurance before God.

8. What is the ultimate purpose of the saving work of God the Father, Son and Holy Spirit (v 6, 12, 14)? The glory of God. God's great aim in saving sinners is to bring to Himself glory and praise.

9. How will God's great purpose ultimately be achieved (v 9-10)? "To bring all things in heaven and earth together under one head, even [ie: especially] Christ" (v 10). This verse tells us that at the centre of the plan of God and all of human history stands not man—not you and me—but the man—Jesus Christ.

This is the mystery (something that was once hidden to the world) that is now revealed to God's people. The great plan of God is to bring to Himself praise and glory through the work of His dear Son, and He is working to bring everything together under His rule at the end of history. God has demonstrated at one and the same time both His perfect love and grace through the crucifixion and resurrection of Jesus, and the supremacy of Jesus Christ over all things. That the supreme Sovereign of all can be humiliated, beaten and killed for the lowest sinners and, at the same time, exalt Himself above all powers is truly reason to glorify God!

- **How do you think the church fits into God's great plan?** The place of the church in the plan of God is one of the great truths revealed through Paul in this letter. What God will do at the end of history throughout all creation, He is doing now as He saves sinners in Christ and unites them together into the church—one body under the headship of Christ (4 v 15).

10. What is Paul's response—and what should be ours—to the amazing truth that Christians have "every spiritual blessing in Christ" (v 3, 14)? Paul, leading the way by example (v 3, 14), wants us to praise God. It's not just our duty as His creatures, but our fitting response to what He is like and what He has done. God blesses us and so we praise Him.

11. APPLY: What does a lack of praising God in our lives show us about ourselves? This question challenges people to think about how often or little and how easily or not they give thought to praising God. People may find it hard to remember to praise God in their own personal prayer times. When praying with other Christians, they may have difficulty joining in a time of praise because they don't know what to say. Paul links his praise of God with understanding that he has received "every spiritual blessing in Christ" (v 3) and all that God the Father, Son and Spirit have done for Christians (v 14). In other words, praising God comes easily to those who understand the gospel. If we are slow to praise God, we need to learn (again, if necessary) what He has done for us.

12. APPLY: How should God's great purpose for our world shape your priorities in life? And those of your church? If we understand that the purpose of all creation and history is to bring glory to God through the person and work of Jesus, our priority—individually and as a church—must be to demonstrate who Jesus is, what He has done and why everyone needs to be in Christ. Our lives and our churches will be Christ-centred. Sharing the glory and grace of Jesus Christ is what God put the church in business to do. Can you think of a better thing to give your life to than showing the supremacy of Jesus Christ in all things?

⌄

- **What things are often at the centre of our lives and churches in place of Christ?** For individual Christians: family, education, career, financial security, comfort, reputation, success. For churches: tradition, numbers, prosperity, reputation, an exciting and innovative programme.

Note: At the end of the session remind people of what was discussed in Session 1, Q1. Compare what you have learned about God's church from 1 v 1-14 eg: church = people who have been blessed by God with every spiritual blessing in Christ etc.

3 Ephesians 1 v 15-23
EYES OPENED BY THE SPIRIT

THE BIG IDEA

The people of Christ's new community are those who have faith in Jesus and love for the saints, but who also grow in knowing God better and understanding the spiritual blessings we have in Christ, as the Spirit opens our eyes to see God's truth.

SUMMARY

Paul moves from praise for what God has done for His people to prayer for the ongoing work of the Spirit in the lives of the Ephesian Christians. He has heard about their faith in the Lord Jesus and their love for all the saints—two defining characteristics of Christ's people—and his prayer is that they will continue to grow—another defining characteristic of true Christians.

Christians grow through the work of the Holy Spirit—"the Spirit of wisdom and revelation" (v 17)—who enlightens or opens the eyes of our hearts. As a result of the Spirit's work, we come to know God better and understand more deeply the spiritual blessings we already have in Christ: the Christian hope we've been called to, the inheritance that awaits us and the God's incomparable power working on our behalf.

Christ's people are different from all other people because we can see by faith the truth of God; in particular, the glory, authority and supremacy of Christ. This God-given ability to see with the eyes of the heart is one of the main differences between Christians and non-Christians.

Practically, this passage has much to teach us about how to pray. We also learn about our attitude and responsibility towards those who are still spiritually blind, and the implications for our everyday lives of Christ's headship over all things.

OPTIONAL EXTRA

What would it be like to be blind? Get your group to imagine one day waking up totally blind. What problems would they face? How would their lives have to change? How would they feel and why? Then read together 2 Corinthians 4 v 4 and see if people can explain why the New Testament describes non-Christians as blind. In this session we see how the Holy Spirit works in the lives of Christians to enlighten or open the eyes of our hearts.

GUIDANCE ON QUESTIONS

1. Imagine meeting and getting to know people in a workplace or social group. How do you think you might recognise a true Christian? What characteristics would you expect to see? Some answers will reveal how much or how little understanding of the gospel there is in your group. As people make suggestions, you could write them on a whiteboard or flipchart. This session highlights three defining characteristics of true Christians: (1) faith in the Lord Jesus Christ; (2) love for all the saints (both covered in questions 2 to 4); (3) growing in the Christian faith through the work of the Spirit (covered in questions 7 to 10). As you come to these questions and find out what Paul considers to be marks of true Christians, refer to your list and highlight those already mentioned, or write them up (separately or in a different colour perhaps) if not on the list.

2. What's the two-part definition of a true Christian or a genuine church given by Paul in verse 15? "Faith in the Lord Jesus" and "love for all God's people".

3. APPLY: In light of Paul's definition, what's the problem with statements like: "I've got faith" or even: "I have faith in God"? A true Christian and a true church has faith "in the Lord Jesus", not just "faith" abstractly or faith in faith (see also v 13). Nor is this faith in a generic idea of "God", without reference to God the Son, Jesus—the one who reveals the Father to us (John 14 v 9). Have you ever noticed how you can talk to practically anyone without fear of offending if you just talk about "God" or "believing" and "faith" instead of talking about Jesus? True faith in God is faith in Jesus, God's Son—without Him all other attempts at knowing God are fruitless.

4. APPLY: And what's the problem with being a lone Christian? If we have true love for Jesus, then we will have true love for the people that Jesus loves—for "ALL Gods people" (v 15; see also John 13 v 34-35). Jesus loves all believers, and so do His people. But you can't do that as a lone Christian. It's in the context of a local church, where we care for one another, that the mutual love that Jesus commands is clearly seen. It's as we love each other—rejoicing with those who rejoice and bearing the burdens of those who weep—that we show the world we are followers of Jesus.

5. Look at *how* Paul prays for the Ephesian Christians in verses 16-19. What principles can you find that should shape our prayers as well?
a. Paul prays with thanksgiving (v 16). He gives God thanks for their redemption and salvation through faith in Christ. That kind of

thanksgiving keeps us centred on the gospel and encouraged as we remind ourselves of the work of grace that God has performed in the lives of loved ones.
b. Paul prays for these Christians continually—"I have not stopped" (v 16) and "I keep asking" (v 17). Instead of praying once or twice and then forgetting about them, his love for them means they stay at the forefront of his mind.
c. When Paul prays for them he has spiritual purposes in mind—that they may know God better (v 17), that their hearts may be enlightened (v 18), and that they may know both the Christian hope and God's almighty power at work in them (v 18-19). He understands that their greatest needs can only be met in Christ and their greatest good can only be found in Him.
d. Paul tells them that he is praying for them. Letting other people know you're praying for them is very encouraging. And notice that Paul goes on to tell them exactly how he is praying for them.

6. APPLY: How do our prayers for each other compare with Paul's example here? Encourage your group to respond to shortcomings in this area by learning from the apostle Paul, rather than simply feeling guilty. We often fall short of Paul's example here because… we don't pray at all for each other or we only pray sporadically; we pray in response to crises or problems rather than regularly and purposefully; we ask for God's help but forget to thank Him for other Christians; we pray more easily about people's physical or financial welfare than their spiritual welfare; we pray for people but don't tell them we are doing so (or we promise to pray for people and then fail to).

• **How can we encourage each other to**

pray more biblically? Get your group to share ideas that will be helpful to them. These may include: preserving the prayer time in this particular group, so that you actually spend 30 minutes praying rather than talking or sharing; encouraging people to make a prayer request for their spiritual wellbeing, rather than their health or other circumstances; restricting parts of your prayer time to a particular theme eg: thanksgiving, asking for boldness in witnessing, asking for joy in difficult situations (get people to write out a brief prayer beforehand if this is helpful); setting up prayer triplets etc.

7. What does Paul pray for the Ephesian Christians in verse 17? Why? Paul asks that God the Father would give the Ephesian Christians "the Spirit of wisdom and revelation". The purpose of the request is so that they may know God better. Knowing God better is achieved through the work of the Holy Spirit revealing God to us. Notice how Paul calls Him "the Spirit of wisdom and revelation".

8. Find three things in verses 18-19 that Paul wants Christians to know.

• The hope to which God has called Christians: "Hope" = the desire for something good along with the expectation of finding it. "Called"— Christians are called to "every spiritual blessing [redemption, wisdom, righteousness, sanctification, glory…] in Christ" (v 3). Paul wants Christians to understand better that they can confidently expect a richly blessed eternal life.

• The riches of God's glorious inheritance in the saints: This could mean either the inheritance that we have from God, now

that we are sons of God, or that God's people (Christians) themselves are God's inheritance. Paul wants us to understand better that they are God's people and His precious possession.

• God's incomparably great power for us who believe: The power that God has for believers is unrivalled—"incomparably great". God is ALL-powerful, and for those who have faith in Jesus Christ, He has promised to use that incomparably great power on our behalf. This is really the peak of these verses. Paul lays great stress on God's power demonstrated publicly and historically in Jesus' resurrection, and now at work in the believer. God's power is resurrection power, ascension power, and ruling power.

• **How do we come to know these things?** For Christians to truly know these things, Paul asks that "the eyes of [their] heart[s] may be enlightened". He is praying that their understanding—minds, thoughts, imagination—would receive light and be illuminated. Paul understands that Christians see with the "eyes" of their hearts, that is, with their inmost being. It means we see beyond this world into the next. This is the work of the Holy Spirit.

9. If the Ephesian Christians already have "every spiritual blessing in Christ", why does Paul need to continually pray for their spiritual wellbeing, do you think? He wants them to grow in their knowledge of them. Something may belong to us, but if we don't know about it or we have forgotten about it, we can't enjoy it and the way we live may be very different as a result. You could illustrate this with the story of Thelma Howard, who for many years was employed as a maid by Walt Disney. Every Christmas he gave her an envelope with a document inside. Because she didn't understand what she had been given, she simply put the envelopes in a safe place and forgot about them. After her death her relatives discovered the gifts were shares in Disney Corporation worth millions.

10. Paul's prayers reveal another defining mark of true Christians (see v 17). What is it? True Christians are those who grow in the faith. Seeing spiritually, with the eyes of the heart, isn't just something that happens once when we become believers. We grow clearer in our understanding of the faith and deeper in our knowledge of God. John Stott has said: "Knowledge is the ladder by which faith climbs higher". John Calvin explained it this way: "Whatever may be the height of our attainments, let them be always accompanied by the desire of something higher". The Holy Spirit is "the Spirit of wisdom and revelation" (v 17), who opens the "eyes" of our hearts so that we can see spiritual realities by faith, as clearly as we see physical objects with our physical eyes.

⌄

- **How should this affect the way we live?** Christians should always be eager to learn more, grow more and understand more of the Christian faith. Encourage people to think about how they might need to change their attitude to Bible teaching in church meetings, Bible studies, Bible-reading partnerships and other opportunities to encourage and be encouraged in their Christian faith.
  And Christians need to pray for the work of the Holy Spirit in their lives to open the eyes of their hearts, both as individuals and as a church.
- **How are you doing in getting to know God better?** So many in Christian circles neglect getting to know God and

enjoy Him. They seem uninterested in God, even bored with Him, when in fact the purpose for which we have been saved and the privilege we now have as the people of God is to enjoy Him forever in all His glory. There is something wrong if a person claims to be a Christian and yet is not growing in their knowledge of God. We don't grow continuously—there are peaks and plateaus. But over the span of our life, there should be evidence that we're maturing in Christ if we are in Him.

11. How do Christians now "see" Christ (v 20-21)? Christ...
- has been raised from the dead—He is physically, and not just spiritually, alive.
- has been seated at God's right hand—a picture of the honour, and exalted rule of Jesus (see Psalm 110 v 1).
- has been given rule over every other power—Jesus rules the entire universe, seen and unseen, material and spiritual.
- has had all things placed under His feet—He even rules over His enemies.
- has been appointed head over everything—compare 1 v 10.

All of this has already been accomplished by the power of God when He raised Jesus from the dead (see Acts 2 v 32-33). But while Jesus does rule and have authority over everything, we are told elsewhere in the NT that His final and complete rule has not yet come (see 1 Corinthians 15 v 26; Hebrews 2 v 8). The final consummation of all things is yet to come.

12. Where does the church fit in God's great plan (v 22-23)? God "appointed him to be head over everything for the church". Though Christ is head over all things, there is a special connection between Him and His gathered people. He fills the church, His body, with His presence by His Spirit (v 23). The church is like a cup that is being filled up with the glorious presence of Jesus her Lord. To understand what v 23 means, compare Colossians 1 v 18-19—Christ, who has the fullness of God dwelling in Him bodily, now dwells in the church, filling God's people with God's glory and power. (Note: Your group may find it difficult to grasp exactly what Paul is saying here, but verses 22-23 should give them some understanding of the exalted status of the church in God's glorious plan. The church is like the "jewel in the crown" of Christ's total rule and authority.)

EXPLORE MORE

Read 1 Corinthians 1 v 18-25. How do non-Christians view the message of Christ crucified? What kind of message do they want? Foolish. Jews wanted miracles; Greeks wanted "wisdom"— eloquence and sophisticated ideas.
How do Christians view the message of Christ crucified? See also verse 30. The wisdom of God, and His power to save them (v 18, 21, 24). **What do you think makes the difference?** People may answer this question superficially—"You have to believe" or "You need to listen to the gospel". While this is true, it doesn't explain what causes some people to believe and others to reject the message. The answer is found in 1 Corinthians 2 v 1-5...
Read 1 Corinthians 2 v 1-5. Paul's message and preaching came with "a demonstration of the Spirit's power" (v 4). What do you think that was? This cannot mean miraculous signs as Paul has just rebuked the Jews for their obsession with miracles and clearly his plain preaching of the gospel did not fit with their views of what God's message should look like (1 v 22-23). Rather, the Spirit's power

is demonstrated in the fact that people come to see the gospel as God's wisdom and power to save them. It is the work of the Spirit in removing spiritual blindness that explains the difference between the Christian's response to Christ and the non-Christian's. This truth humbles us (1 v 31), but also gives us great assurance (2 v 5).

13. APPLY: Non-believers don't have the Holy Spirit working in their lives. In what way, therefore, are they different from Christians? The ability to see with the eyes of the heart, or by faith, is one of the main differences between Christians and non-Christians. For example, Christians recognise Jesus' resurrection as the crowning event of human history and the source of our rescue from God's judgment. Non-Christians only see an ancient myth from a dusty and boring book that has little relevance for today. Compare Ephesians 4 v 18 and 1 Corinthians 2 v 14.

• **What difference will this make to our relationships with them?** We should never envy them because their lives are governed by lies and they are cut off from God. We should not depend on their advice or ideas, without listening to mature fellow Christians as well. We will understand that their greatest need is to hear the gospel of Jesus Christ, and everything that we do with and for them should be for the purpose of sharing about Christ with them. We will pray for them, because we understand that our words, arguments and good deeds can have no effect on them unless the Spirit opens the eyes of their hearts. We will want them to hear God's word, which the Spirit uses to reveal God's truth, and we will do what we can to make that possible.

14. APPLY: What do the truths of verses 19-23 mean for:

• **our personal discipleship?** We seek to live increasingly under Jesus' rule and teaching. We grow in seeing and loving Him as both Saviour and Lord. We aim to believe and follow everything that He believed and taught. And we are to do this in every area of our lives—from decisions about careers and what to study in college, to intimate choices like who we date or marry.

• **our stewardship of what God has given us?** We recognise that everything we have is God's. We aim to use all of our resources (time, gifts, money, energy) for His glory and the promotion of His name. Our great shame would be to do anything with the blessings He has given us that would displease God. And our great joy is to do everything we can with all that we have to do the things that please Him.

• **our church and its leadership/ direction?** Jesus is the head of the church. Fundamentally, we are all joined together to follow Jesus, not human Bible teachers or church leaders, or anyone else. We follow our leaders and teachers as far as they follow Christ and endeavour to display His headship.

• **our involvement in our society?** Christians know the great plan of God in history, so we should endeavour to demonstrate or reflect in public life the exalted rule of Jesus Christ. Christ rules over all and His rule is good. To see His rule reflected in public life is to see the best good done for the greatest number of people. Hopefully, as people see the goodness of God's rule reflected even in human laws, they may choose to turn to Him.

Ephesians 2 v 1-10
4 RAISED WITH CHRIST

THE BIG IDEA
The people of Christ's new community are those who were once dead in sins, but who God has now made alive in Christ, has raised up with Christ, and has created anew in Christ to do good works.

SUMMARY
This session looks at the greatest turnaround story of all—how God saves "dead" sinners to become His workmanship—His new and living people. Outside Christ all people are so corrupted, helpless and hopeless that we are described as "dead" in our sins. This dire predicament is the result of:

• the world around us, whose ways are consistently disobedient to God's ways
• demonic captivity by the evil spirit of the age
• our own internal inclination to sin

Together these are often summarised as the world, the flesh, and the devil.

The turnaround comes in verse 4 with the words "But ... God". What follows is a revelation of God's character—full of "great love", "rich in mercy" and summed up in the phrase "the incomparable riches of his grace"—and then a description of God's saving, life-changing work in Christ. "Dead" sinners are made alive, raised up, seated in heaven and created anew to do good works. And God's purpose in all this is to reveal Himself and be glorified in Jesus Christ.

It's important for Christians to remember what we once were, so that we will never trust in our own efforts or be tempted to boast, but will give thanks and glory to God. It's equally important to remember that we have been not only saved in Christ but created "new" in Him, so that we will live out what we have now become. By doing good in this world we reveal to others the grace and glory of God.

OPTIONAL EXTRA

Ask one or two people to briefly summarise the story of how they became a Christian. Get them to base it on three points:
• What I was once like
• What happened to me
• How I changed
You could use a timer and give people no more than one minute to share their story. This is a useful exercise as real-life opportunities to do this are usually very brief.

GUIDANCE ON QUESTIONS

1. How do you view your past? Is it something you remember fondly? Something you want to forget? How relevant or irrelevant is it to who you are today? The Bible passage in this session outlines the unpalatable truth about the past of every Christian. People don't need to share about their past in any detail. The question should simply get them to think about any tendency they may have to ignore or deny what happened in the past, or conversely, to brood about it and be dominated by it.

2. How does Paul describe the lives of these Ephesian Christians before they came to faith in Jesus (v 1)? "Dead" in their sins. Because our sin cuts us off from God, who is the only source of life, the consequence for us must be spiritual death. **What does Paul's choice of word here tell us about the condition of those who are still outside of Christ?** Can you think of a more desperate condition than "dead"? Not sick, weak, fatigued, or confused... but dead! This is the Bible's diagnosis of the state of all mankind since the fall. Verses 1-3 show that this is true of all of us, and not just these particular Ephesians. Notice the progression in these first three verses: "As for you" (v 1), "all of us" (v 3), "like the rest" (v 3). Paul first addresses his Gentile Christian readers, then moves to "all of us," a reference to himself and other Jewish believers, and finally speaks about "the rest", which includes all of mankind. This desperate condition of spiritual death extends universally to all. All people either were or are dead in their sins.

3. This condition is caused by following what (v 2)? (Find two answers.)
(1) We have "followed the ways of this world". John Stott describes this as the "entire social and value-system of materialism, hedonism, amoral relativism, and God-repudiating secularism". The ways of the world are consistent with disobedience to God. This means that the world's ideas about relationships, children, business, beauty, sex, etc. are all corrupt and lead to death. We once took on board the practices of the world with no suspicion, no resistance, no reflection, no thought for the fact that the end of the world's ways is death.
(2) We have followed the ways of "the ruler of the kingdom of the air". He is "the spirit who is now at work in those who are disobedient"—in other words, God's enemy,

the devil. See also 1 John 3 v 10.

4. Many try to blame their sin on the influence of the world or believe that "the devil made me do it". What's Paul's answer to this in verse 3? The devil tempts us to do the very things we want to do ourselves. As non-Christians we willingly, freely, voluntarily gave ourselves over to satisfying the cravings of our sinful nature, which is never full. Our lustful desires and our thoughts were always for evil. Summary: our sinful human natures are the result of three factors—our internal inclination to sin, external influences from society, and demonic captivity by the evil spirit of the age. "The world, the flesh, and the devil" are powerfully active in the lives of all people.

5. In God's eyes, what is the status of those outside of Christ, and why (v 3)? Paul concludes of anyone outside Christ (including us before we became Christians: "We were by nature deserving of wrath," the wrath of the God of creation. Why? Because of our disobedience to Him. People today tend to disconnect their wrongdoing from any thought of rebellion against God! But our disobedience, our moral failures, our satisfying of sinful cravings and lusts are actions we take against the one holy God of creation. (See Explore More below for a closer look at the link between wrongdoing and rebellion against God.)

🔽

It may be helpful to discuss this question:
• **What is God's wrath like and how is it different to human anger?** God's wrath is not whimsical, petty, or vindictive. He is not vengeful in the way men are vengeful, with their thirst for inflicting pain on others (see 2 Peter 3 v 9b). "For

God so loved the world…" (John 3 v 16). The wrath of God is His righteous, perfect, consistent, unerring, good, holy, God-exalting, account-reckoning, justice-establishing, sovereignty-proving, free-willing response against sin and sinners, who are by nature, by their inner desires, depravity, thoughts, and craving, appropriately deserving of wrath.

EXPLORE MORE
Read Romans 1 v 18-32. The Bible consistently links our wrongdoing with our rebellion against God. What is mankind's attitude to God? Mankind suppresses the truth about God (v 18), even though everyone clearly understands His eternal power and divine nature (v 20). We neither glorify Him nor give thanks to Him (v 21). Instead of worshipping God, we worship created things (v 23, 25).

What behaviour results from this attitude? Darkened and foolish thinking (v 21-22), idolatry (v 23, 25), impure and unnatural sexual relations (v 24, 26-27), and depraved behaviour, affecting our relationships, actions, words, hearts, minds and integrity (v 28-31).

What excuses for our behaviour are demolished in these verses (see v 20 and 32)? We cannot say in our defence that we didn't know there was a God (v 20), or that we didn't know that this kind of behaviour matters to Him (v 32). Paul is convinced that these truths are self-evident to everyone.

Read the verdict of Scripture on human nature in Romans 3 v 10-12. Paul has gathered a number of OT quotations. Notice how "There is no one who does good" (v 12) follows on from "No one … seeks God" (v 11), reflecting the causes and effects outlined in Romans 1 v 18-32.

6. APPLY: Share examples of how this has been true in your life and what changed when you became a Christian. It's good to remind ourselves of how we lived before we came to faith in Christ; and it's a great encouragement for others to hear how we have been changed by the gospel of Jesus Christ. If people are reluctant to share, begin with your own story and give specific examples of how you followed the ways of the world and the devil, from which you have now been rescued. Your story doesn't have to be dramatic—often the most helpful stories are those that "ordinary" people can relate to.

7. Find three words in verses 4-6 that sum up the character of God. What does each one mean for sinful people like us?
(1) Love (v 4): "Because of his great love for us [ie: for Christians]..." It is God's love that compels Him to act and do something about our rebellion and slavery to sin. His wrath is hot and ready, and yet, for those whom He has chosen (1 v 4), He acts—not out of vengeance and justice, which are rightly His, but out of love. We were dead in trespasses and sins, following the world, the devil, and our sinful nature... and yet, He had "great love for us".
(2) Mercy (v 4): Mercy is kindness shown to the guilty. It means not punishing us as our sins deserve. God is "rich" in this mercy. While men chase coins and paper currency, God is a wealthy merchant of mercy.
(3) Grace (v 5): See also verse 8. Compare 1 v 5-8. If mercy = not punishing us as our sins deserve, grace = giving us what we positively do not deserve. It is unmerited, unearned favour in the face of everything we have done to disqualify ourselves for God's kindness. Not only have we not earned God's favour, we have positively

forfeited it because of our sin.

8. Why is it that people generally don't share this view of God's character? (Look at how verses 4-6 follow on from verses 1-3.) The greatness of God's love (v 4-6) is seen most clearly against the greatness of our sins (v 1-3). Many people never meet this God of rich mercy because they are unwilling to admit their sins against God. Hiding their eyes from the obvious truth of their sins, they block out this richly merciful God. We can never find the mercy of God until all of our pretended ignorance of sin and our self-justifying rationalisations are exposed; we must understand that we have nothing to offer God but our sins, and that we need the mercy of God.

9. Find the things that God has done in Christ for His people mentioned in the following verses:
- **v 5:** He has "made us alive with Christ". Verses 1-7 make up one long sentence in the original Greek, with God as the subject and "made us alive" the main verb. When we were helplessly "dead" in our transgressions and sins, God gave us a vitality that we did not have. How does God do this? "With Christ" = through the atoning sacrifice of His Son, Jesus.

- **v 6:** "God raised us up with Christ." The cold grip of spiritual death has already been loosed and one day we will also be free of physical death. God has also "seated us with him in the heavenly realms in Christ Jesus." In Christ our status is now that of sitting next to God in heaven, which is "far above all rule and authority, power and dominion, and every name that is invoked" (1 v 21), and where we are blessed with "every spiritual blessing in Christ" (1 v 3). What God has accomplished in Christ, He has also accomplished in each believer. God's people share in the destiny of their Lord.

- **v 10:** God has "created" us anew "in Christ Jesus". He continues to work in us "to will and to act in order to fulfil his good purpose" (Phil 2 v 13) ie: to want and to carry out what He wants us to do. Verse 10 says: "We are God's handiwork"—His work of art or masterpiece. The beauty we defiled and rejected, we can now demonstrate in the new life God has given us.

⌄

- **Make the connections between our predicament outside Christ and God's merciful intervention.** Verses 1 and 5: We were dead in sins… but now God has made us alive in Christ through faith. Verses 2 and 6: We were once ruled by Satan… but now God has raised us and seated us in the heavenly realms where we rule with Christ. Verses 3 and 10: We once gratified our sinful nature… but now we walk in good deeds prepared by God for us to do.

10. What is God's ultimate purpose in our salvation (v 7)? Verse 7 must be the most overlooked verse in this passage. God saves the people He loves "in order that in the coming ages he might show the incomparable riches of his grace, expressed in his kindness to us in Christ Jesus." God's great aim is to be glorified in His creation by revealing Himself in Christ Jesus. (See also 1 v 12.)

11. What is incompatible with God's grace (v 8-9)? God's grace in Christ is wholly incompatible with any human merit or work, and therefore with any boasting on our part. We can only trust in what Jesus

Christ has done for us, and even that faith is a gracious gift of God. And how could it be otherwise? Dead men don't believe and they don't work. They don't do anything other than rot in their graves! A boastful Christian is an anomaly—a self-contradiction. It's doubtful whether a boastful Christian can be a Christian at all since he/she clearly doesn't understand God's grace (see v 8).

12. APPLY: Ephesians 2 v 1-10 helps us understand what it is to be a true Christian. From these verses work out some of the characteristics that you would expect to find in a true Christian. Rather than accept at face value a person's claim to be a Christian, we should expect those who claim to be Christians to show characteristics compatible with God's work in their lives. For example: humbly admitting our sinfulness (v 1-3); accepting that God is right to be angry with us (v 3); understanding that there is nothing we can do to save ourselves and trusting in Christ to do that for us (v 5); refusing to boast in any "goodness" of our own and instead giving all the glory to God (v 9, 7); living in this world to do God's good works (v 10). A true Christian divides their life into two parts—the time when they were outside Christ and dead, and the time when God included them in Christ and made them alive.

13. APPLY: If you are a Christian, the love, mercy and grace of God has already come to you. The question is: how can you live more fully in recognition of His grace? Think about the difference God's grace to you will make in the following areas of your life:
- **Your view of your sins:** Remember them often—but never without thinking of God's work in your life. Embrace the past tense nature of these acts of God. You are

free from sin, sin's penalty, and the grip of death. So, don't be paralysed by the fear of sin. Realise you are free from any self-imposed standard of perfection. Christ is your perfection and you are free in Him. Use and delight in your freedom, for the glory of God and the blessing of others and yourself.

- **The way you treat others:** Treat others with grace, remembering what you were

and how God's grace was your only hope. Strive to help your church become a community marked by grace, love, and mercy, in the likeness of God's own character.

- **Your part in the work God has given His people:** Remember what you once were, live out what you now are, and do the work of an evangelist.

5 Ephesians 2 v 11-22
UNITED IN CHRIST

THE BIG IDEA

Christ's new community are from diverse and even hostile groups who have been reconciled with God through faith in Christ. They are now united into one kingdom, family and temple belonging to God.

SUMMARY

In the second half of Ephesians 2 Paul repeats the basic message of verses 1-10 but adds a new dimension of ethnic division, exclusion and strife. He moves from addressing the Ephesian believers as individuals to speaking about them as an ethnic group—Gentiles, as distinct from Jews. Paul addresses this section to "you who are Gentiles by birth and called 'uncircumcised' by those who call themselves 'the circumcision'". The address itself points to the ethnic alienation that his readers were facing.

Paul's message here is that, in Christ, even a division as hostile, intractable and long-standing as that between Jew and Gentile is broken down, as those who are far away from God are brought near to Him by the

gospel of peace. Gentiles are equal with the Jews—given access to the Father by the one Spirit, and recreated with the Jews as one new kind of man—a citizen of the kingdom of God. Gentiles—who were once estranged from God's people, God's promises, and God Himself—can now be united with other believers as citizens of God's kingdom, members of God's household or family, and the "living stones" of God's new temple, where God Himself dwells.

All this means that true Christians are united and can be at peace with all other true Christians, regardless of race, ethnicity, class, age, gender, or any other division found in human societies. It means too that the message of Jesus Christ is the only solution to the lack of peace that we find at every level in our world. This session challenges us to find and promote peace with God and others through the gospel alone, and to live out in our churches our unity in Christ with Christians of all backgrounds.

OPTIONAL EXTRA

How diverse is your church? Make a list

together of all the different groups that are represented in your church—the list can include nationalities or ethnic groups, age-ranges etc. One of the things this will do is to highlight how well you know your church. Then think about your local community. Are there any groups of people who are not represented or are under-represented in your church? You could discuss why that might be so and what could be done to reach and welcome people from these groups. You may discover that your church has a considerable diversity of people, and that will be a great illustration of the main teaching point in this session. Or you may find that your church is largely made up of people from a similar background, in which case there will be some practical challenges to take on board.

GUIDANCE ON QUESTIONS

1. Identify some groups in your community, area or nation that don't get on, and some of the conflicts that have resulted from these divisions. These may be based on race and ethnicity, religion, social class, income, political affiliation, age, or culture and lifestyle (eg: in rural areas traditional farming communities versus affluent and liberal incomers relocating out of cities). You may even have divisions like this in your own church. **What solutions are often suggested and how successful are they?** Popular solutions put forward by politicians and community leaders include: education (especially for children), investment, political power sharing, social engineering, community events, and political correctness. The success of these solutions is bound to be limited because none of them deal with our estrangement from God, which is the root cause of our estrangement from one another.

2. What words and phrases describe the status and experience of the Gentiles before they were included in Christ?
- Gentiles (v 11)
- uncircumcised (v 11)
- separate from Christ (v 12)
- excluded from citizenship (v 12)
- foreigners to the covenants of the promise (v 12)
- without hope (v 12)
- without God (v 12)
- far away (v 13)

The term "Gentile" is used throughout Scripture to refer to non-Jews. Circumcision was the sign of God's covenant with His people. So to be called "uncircumcised" was to be called pagan or heathen. The situation of the Gentiles was desperate. The basic descriptions are terrible enough, but when we add the specific detail it is hard to think of a more desolate and hopeless condition: "separate" from the Messiah—the promised Deliverer and Saviour of men from their sins (v 1-10); "excluded" from citizenship in Israel—that is, shut out from those God chose as the objects of His special love; "foreigners to the covenants of the promise"—the blood oath of God to make for Himself a special people and to be their loving and merciful God. Gentiles were estranged from God's people, God's promises, and God Himself.

3. How does Paul view those of Jewish birth? (What do you think is meant by his comment in verse 11 about "the circumcision"?) It wasn't only Gentiles who were alienated from God, but even people of Jewish background. That seems to be what's hinted at in Paul's statement at the end of verse 11: "the circumcision" (which is done in the body by human hands)". Paul is pointing out that the Jews bore the sign of a relationship with God outwardly only. Their physical foreskins were cut by the hands of men, but there was no sign in their hearts of a living relationship with God. So although they had known all the advantages of being born in the right nation and being raised in the correct kind of religious family, they too were separated from God.

4. What has now been done for these Gentiles, and how (v 13)? They have been brought near. They were once excluded and separated but now are brought near, brought into a new nation made of Jew and Gentile. The old disadvantages caused by birth and religion have been overcome. *How?* This nearness is "in Christ". In other words, the nearness we can have with God is found through union with His Son. "In Christ" was the new identity that overcame their exclusion and separation. They were no longer Jews and non-Jews; they were now "Christians" ("Christ"-ians)—members of a new, spiritual "ethnic" group. It is not ethnic origin, ancestry, or religious upbringing that matters but whether or not we are included in Christ.

5. What is Paul emphasising in verse 14 when he says: "he himself"? Peace is found in one Person only. Jesus is the only peace available to Jew and Gentile alike. The fact that Jesus is our peace rules out other false sources of peace. Peace is not about public policy, military might, education or philosophy, or inner strength, or anything else outside of Christ.

6. What four things has Jesus has done to bring us peace?
- **v 14:** Jesus has made "the two groups one". In Christ, those who were ethnically Jews and those who had come from a completely different ethnic origin were now united into a new "ethnic" group—God's kingdom.

- **v 14:** Jesus has "destroyed the barrier, the dividing wall of hostility". This barrier is the symbol of all that separated Jew from Gentile. Some commentators think that this has special reference to the temple of Herod in Jerusalem, which featured just such a dividing wall. This wall surrounded and separated the inner temple (which only Jewish people could enter) from the outer court, or Court of the Gentiles. It meant that Gentiles could see the temple but could not approach it. (See Paul's experience in Acts 21 v 27-29.) However, in this context (see v 15) the dividing wall of hostility is probably best understood as the law with its commandments and regulations. That law separated Israel from all who were outsiders. It marked them out as different, and eventually became the source of much pride.

- **v 15a:** Jesus has abolished the law with its commandments and regulations. This doesn't mean that the moral law has been abolished. Right and wrong remain for both Jew and Gentile. Jesus fulfilled the moral law through His perfect obedience (Romans 5 v 19), and so, for those who are in Christ, the righteous requirements of the law have been met (Romans 8 v 1-4). What was abolished was the penalty of that law through His sacrifice on the cross. But He also fulfilled—and therefore abolished or made obsolete—the civil law and customs of Israel. Those laws taught a ceremonial cleanness through the sacrificial system and divided Jew from Gentile. But those laws were merely pointers to the true cleansing sacrifice of Christ, when the people of God were purified from their sins.

- **v 17:** Jesus has preached peace to both Jew and Gentile. On one level, this could be how Paul here chooses to summarise

Jesus' earthly ministry. At another level, this can also be a description of the ministry of Paul and his co-workers to those, like these Ephesian Gentiles, who had now come to faith in Christ. Paul and the other apostles were continuing the ministry of Jesus by preaching the peace of the gospel to both Jews and Gentiles (see v 20).

EXPLORE MORE
… Read Luke 2 v 8-14; 19 v 41-44; John 14 v 27; 16 v 33. What do we learn here about the peace of the gospel?
Luke 2 v 8-14: When Jesus was born, the angels proclaimed a message of God's favour and peace coming to men.
Luke 19 v 41-44: Later, when Jesus triumphantly entered Jerusalem on a donkey (itself a sign of peace: see Zechariah 9 v 9-10), the Jewish leaders refused to recognise that the means of peace—their long-awaited Messiah—had come to them (see v 37-39).
John 14 v 27; 16 v 33: But for His disciples, those who heard the message and believed, Jesus had words that reassured them of His peace. Notice however, that this would not be peace instead of troubles, but peace in troubles.

7. APPLY: Based on what you have learned so far, how could you respond to people who say the following:
a. "We'll never have world peace until we all teach our children properly to respect and value all people equally." It is a common fallacy today to believe that we only need better education to solve problems like racism and hatred of people different from ourselves. The problem is that simply knowing what is right and wrong doesn't give us the power to do what's right and reject

what's wrong. The verdict of the Bible is very different: we'll never have world peace until we have all been reconciled with God.
b. "Religion is what causes war, so Christianity can never be the answer to hatred and division." Any religion—even those that call themselves "Christian"—not based on the revelation of God in the Bible is an invention of human minds. So we should not be surprised that religions cause wars. But the message of Jesus Christ revealed in the Bible is utterly different: it's not a human invention but the revelation of God Himself (1 Corinthians 2 v 6-10). Only the message of Jesus Christ can answer the hatred and divisions that tear apart the human race.
c. "I believe we have to find peace in our own hearts before we can expect to have world peace." This comment is partly right. However, people who say this kind of thing often do not understand what the problem of the human heart really is. "Finding peace in our own hearts" usually means something like accepting ourselves with all our faults, forgiving ourselves for past failings, etc. God is rarely brought into the picture, and beliefs about sin, guilt and judgment are seen as positively harmful to inner peace. But the Bible teaches that the problem of the human heart is our wilful rebellion against God, and the only solution is the atoning death of Jesus on the cross.

8. What did Jesus do in order to make peace (v 15b-16)? Jesus' purpose was to create one new kind of man out of the two hostile groups represented by the Jews and the Gentiles. He did this by bringing both "sides" to peace with God through one means—the cross. Equal before God in need and blessing, they are now able to be at peace with each other, seeing the other "group" as equal. This kind of inter-racial unity cannot be produced by human ideas or institutions —it is God's handiwork (2 v 10).

9. Find two things that characterise Christ's new creation:

- **v 15:** Reconciliation with fellow Christians: "Horizontal" unity is only made possible through "vertical" reconciliation. But where vertical reconciliation truly exists, horizontal unity is inevitable. Christ's people are able to do what no other group can—to live in peace with God and each other, regardless of our diverse backgrounds.

- **v 16 and 18:** Reconciliation with God: Neither the privileges of Israel nor the disadvantages of the Gentiles changed the fundamental problem of our hearts' hostility toward God, demonstrated by our sins. The cross didn't just make something possible or potentially possible; it achieved the purposes of God—reconciliation between man and man, and between man and God. Verse 18 says we have access to the Father: notice the fullness of God made available to us—God the Son dying for our peace, opening access to God the Father, through fellowship with God the Spirit.

10. What three pictures illustrate Christ's community and our part in it?

- **v 19:** Citizenship. Having new life in Christ means that we become citizens of the kingdom of heaven.

- **v 19:** Members of God's household. It's not just that we've made it inside the borders of a new kingdom, but by God's

grace we have been brought into the King's household—and not as servants but as family members and heirs.

- **v 22:** God's dwelling. We are the house or dwelling of God. All God's people of all time through faith in Jesus Christ have become the temple of God indwelled by the Holy Spirit of God. (See Revelation 21 v 3.)

11. What do v 20-22 tell us about the foundation of Christ's new community?

We are "built on the foundation of the apostles and prophets"—not on the men themselves, but on their message. Their teachings are foundational to the Christian church. That's why every form of "Christianity" that attacks the teachings of the apostles crumbles and fails. And Christ Jesus Himself is the chief cornerstone. The message preached by the NT apostles and the prophets could be summarised as "Christ Jesus" (see 1 Corinthians 1 v 23; 2 v 2; 2 Peter 1 v 16; 1 John 1 v 1-2).

12. APPLY: What difference does this passage make to your understanding of the Christian church? (1) Christianity is far more corporate than we're accustomed to thinking. It's not all about a personal relationship with Christ. Yes, individuals must repent of their sins and place their trust in Christ to be saved. But Christ saves people to make them into a new community—a kingdom, a household, a building—where people no longer relate to each other according to history, culture, race or tradition, but live out their unity in Christ. (2) This passage promises far greater unity than we might imagine. It speaks directly to unity across racial and ethnic lines. This should make us zealous in our pursuit of multi-ethnic and class unity in the church. It tells us plainly that racism is completely

incompatible with following Jesus. The gospel of Jesus Christ is powerful enough to turn racists into those who love others regardless of their origin. It creates bonds where there were none and unity where there were only gulfs.

13. APPLY: In what practical ways will this teaching affect how you live, both individually and as a church? Allow the group to share any thoughts and ideas about practical application that they may have, or discuss the following suggestions.
(1) We should be an energetically inclusive community—our aim should be to find the strangers and aliens among us and see that they are reconciled to us and most importantly to God.
(2) We should encourage, support and join with those involved in ministering to the strangers or foreigners among us—economic migrants, expatriate workers, international students, asylum seekers etc, as well as those groups who are easily over-looked, like the homeless, the physically disabled or learning disabled, residents of socially deprived areas, the illiterate, the elderly, disaffected youth etc.
(3) We should be hospitable and welcoming every time we meet together. Rather than hanging out with friends, make an effort to greet visitors, welcome strangers and get to know newcomers.
(4) Let's discover and enjoy our diversity—by talking about our ethnic backgrounds, sharing our different kinds of food, music etc, listening to one another and all the while encouraging each other in Christ, who has made all of us one in Him and has destroyed our enmity.

6 Ephesians 3
GIVEN GOD'S MESSAGE

THE BIG IDEA
God shows the universe His wisdom through the way His new community serves the gospel and prays for each other.

SUMMARY
Through the gospel of peace preached to both Jews and Gentiles, God has created a new kind of man and a new community. In chapter 3 we learn more from Paul about the message of this gospel of peace and the task of being God's messenger.

Paul describes himself as an apostle of Christ Jesus, a role that is foundational to the church, so therefore unique and which cannot be replicated in our day. But he also describes himself as a servant of the gospel and a prisoner of Christ Jesus. As God's messenger, Paul exemplifies humility, gratitude for God's grace and willingness to suffer—characteristics that we too should demonstrate as we proclaim the same gospel.

Paul describes God's message as the mystery of Christ—a mystery because it cannot be discovered by human intellect, investigation, or research—but now God has revealed to His apostles the astounding truth that, in Christ, Jews and Gentiles together will be the people of God. This seems contrary to all of God's separating and dividing activity in Old Testament Israel, but God has brought about something no one could have anticipated, and thus demonstrates His unique wisdom and glory. It's through seeing the church and what God has done in the lives of believers that the spiritual forces of darkness understand God's supremacy.

This understanding of the importance of the church prompts Paul to pray a remarkable prayer for the Ephesians. He wants them to keep growing as a Christ-centred and Christ-witnessing community. The importance of believers joining a church, and thinking about how we proclaim the gospel to the world, are the main points of application.

OPTIONAL EXTRA

Challenge the group to come up with a text message or "tweet" of less than 140 characters that explains the essence of the gospel. If group members have mobile phones with them, make it a race to send it to you with prizes for the fastest/best.

GUIDANCE ON QUESTIONS

1. How do you feel about talking about the Christian faith with others? What do you struggle with? What gives you encouragement? This session focuses on the message of the gospel and Christ's people as messengers of the gospel. This is not an easy task to carry out in our secular, cynical and pleasure-obsessed society. Proclaiming the gospel must always involve a willingness to suffer—it did for Paul, and we can expect no less. But hopefully people will find it helpful to learn that they are not alone in struggling with fear of rejection, embarrassment, inability to find the right words etc. Help your group to look forward to being encouraged by what Paul says in this passage about God's message and the job of being His messenger.

2. Find three ways in which Paul describes himself as a messenger of God in these verses. What does each one tell us about this role?
- **v 1:** "The prisoner of Christ Jesus". Paul was in prison in Rome when he wrote this letter (compare 6 v 20). In fact, he was frequently imprisoned for preaching the gospel. God's messengers must be willing to suffer. Our role is to devote our lives to faithfully defending and proclaiming what the Lord says. Whether it goes well or badly, we can trust the results to the Lord.

- **v 5 (also 1 v 1):** "An apostle of Christ Jesus". Apostles are literally "messengers" or "sent ones". Paul didn't promote himself to the office of apostle—he was called and set apart (see Romans 1 v 1; Galatians 1 v 1). "Apostles" are people who carry a message by a sender and, therefore, go with the authority of the sender. Similarly, "prophets" are those who speak the very words of God. Paul speaks what he has been given from above, revealed by the Holy Spirit (v 5). (Note: Apostles and prophets are foundational in the church (2 v 20). At this special point in history, men like Paul were chosen and moved by God to speak His message in a unique, authoritative, and infallible way, and in this sense, the office and function of apostle and prophet are no longer continuing. This is clearly demonstrated by the "qualifications" required for apostleship—see Acts 1 v 21-22.)

- **v 7:** "A servant of this gospel". Notice that Paul is a servant "by the gift of God's grace". In other words, Paul did not earn this privileged position eg: by completing special training for it at university. Nor did he deserve it—Paul recognised that he was unworthy even to be a servant (v 8). As someone has said: "God does not call the qualified; He qualifies the called". "Servant", therefore, is the right self-description when your position is one given to you by grace. Being selected by God's grace should make the messenger humble, not proud or arrogant. Most people want to be thought of as a servant but they don't actually want to be (or be treated like) servants. Paul was a great man of undoubted gifts and abilities, but he knew his place. He welcomed this humble station as "the gift of God's grace" that it was.

3. How does Paul describe the gospel message in verse 3, and why (v 5)?
As "the mystery made known to me by revelation" (v 3). A "mystery" in Scripture is something that has been hidden but now is made known or revealed. Men of previous generations have not understood and so have not been able to proclaim the message that Paul now proclaims (v 5).

4. What is the "mystery" about (v 4-6)?
Christ (v 4). That is what was not made known to men in other generations (v 5). However, it was revealed by the Spirit to God's apostles and prophets in New Testament times. The men of the Old Testament had glimpses and saw traces of the Christ (= Messiah). But since Christ has come, these have been revealed in full. Verse 6 tells us more fully what the mystery is:
• Jews and Gentiles are heirs together.
• Jews and Gentiles are members together of one body (see also 2 v 14-17).
• Jews and Gentiles are sharers together in the promise in Christ Jesus.

5. How do people come to understand the mystery of the gospel (v 4-5, 8-10)? Through whom and by which means?

The mysteries of God must be shown to us by God Himself. First, it has been revealed to God's holy apostles and prophets (v 5)—men like Paul—who have written it down (v 4), preached it (v 8) and worked at making it plain to everyone (v 9). After the foundational period of the apostles and prophets, God's message is revealed to the world through the church (v 10) proclaiming the teaching of the apostles. For us today this means that we can come to understand the mystery of Christ through—and only through—the reading and teaching of God's word, the Bible, by servants of the gospel in Bible-believing churches.

6. The mystery of the gospel was something that even the greatest minds could not have discovered in Old Testament times. Why would this mystery (see v 6) be so surprising back then?
The result of Christ's messiahship—the establishment of a new kingdom of God's people made up of both Jews and Gentiles united in Christ—seems contrary to all of God's separating and dividing activity in Old Testament Israel. Everywhere God separated Israel from Gentiles by His law and His word. But now, He is uniting them in one body. The promises of God were not limited to Israel. This was something that even the apostles needed convincing about (see Acts 11 v 1-18). This mystery turned everyone's world upside down! God was bringing about something that no one had anticipated.

7. How does the mystery of the gospel—Christ's new community—become a reality (v 6)?
Jews and Gentiles are united "through the gospel". This is interesting and profoundly important. The message itself brings about the fulfilment of the mystery. Not only does the message

say something, but it also has power! (See Romans 1 v 16.)

EXPLORE MORE
Read Matthew 28 v 18-20; Colossians 4 v 2-6; 1 Peter 3 v 15-16 ... what do these New Testament passages teach us about the role of all Christians in proclaiming the gospel?
• Matthew 28 v 18-20: Jesus is clearly addressing the whole church since Jesus talks about making disciples of "all nations" and promises His presence with His servants "to the very end of the age". The task involves teaching people everything that Christ has commanded us.
• Colossians 4 v 2-6: There's a division of labour here with some Christians given the task of praying for others, like Paul, whose role is to proclaim the gospel. Specifically, they are instructed to pray for opportunities for the gospel and for clear communication on the part of the evangelists. But notice that those who serve by praying for teachers and evangelists should also make the most of every opportunity that comes their way, and know how to answer people around them who have queries about the gospel.
• 1 Peter 3 v 13-16: The instructions here are set in the context of suffering. Christ's people should continue to follow and obey Him, whatever the cost. When this provokes questions, they should speak gently and respectfully about the gospel and make sure that their lives reflect their words.

8. APPLY: How does Paul's totally God-centred view of the gospel compare with the way the Christian faith is often understood and proclaimed today?
Discuss how the way we speak about the gospel or share the story of how we became a Christian can give a very different impression to Paul's humble, God-centred

perspective. The gospel and our response to it comes entirely from the hands of God.

9. Why has God, through the gospel, created the church (v 10-11)? To reveal His wisdom to the spiritual realm. In other words, when the spiritual authorities and powers see the church, they cannot be in any doubt about the surpassing greatness of God's wisdom in all that He has done for His people. Notice that this is not simply a hope in the mind of God—something that only might happen. It has been accomplished in Christ Jesus our Lord (v 11). Through the church God announces the defeat of the spiritual forces of darkness.

10. How do the following things feature in Paul's prayer for the Ephesians?
• **strength:** Paul prays that God will strengthen the Ephesians out of His own resources and power, through the work of His Spirit in their hearts (v 16). In other words, this is a supernatural strength that can only be given by God. The result of being given this strength is that Christ lives in them by faith (v 17).

• **love:** This isn't just a superficial belief that "God is love" but a profound, life-changing conviction on which they can build their assurance of salvation and hope of eternal life, and which will spur them on to live as God's people whatever may come their way.

• **faith:** That is, trust in the character of God and the saving work of Christ. Through faith they will have the presence of Christ Himself in their hearts and lives (v 17).

• **understanding:** The implication here is that there is always more for us to learn and understand about Christ's love. We never reach the end of growing in faith.

• **knowledge:** Since love is not a doctrine

but a quality expressed in relationship, Paul must be praying that they will experience the love of Christ—that they will feel and enjoy and celebrate His love for them.

- **God the Father:** It is the Father that Paul comes to in prayer, in humility on his knees (v 14) and in reverence for who He is (v 15), but also with confidence that God has abundant resources and power to strengthen His people (v 16). But more than that, Paul wants the impossible for the Ephesians—he wants them to be filled with the fullness of God (v 19).

- **Christ:** Paul longs for Christ to dwell in the hearts of His people (v 17) and he knows that it is understanding and experiencing the love of Christ that keeps these Christians rooted and established. His goal is that they are Christ-centred and Christ-witnessing people.

- **the Holy Spirit:** It is not just words—even gospel words—that change and grow God's people, but the supernatural work of God the Holy Spirit that comes through the teaching of God's word.

- **What do you imagine Christians would be like as a result of this prayer?** Let your group describe in real-life terms, in your own context, the Christian that would be the result of God answering this prayer.

11. APPLY: Jesus has given to His church the task of proclaiming the gospel to all nations. From what you learned in this session, what is your part in that? Help people see the many different ways in which they can join in the task of proclaiming the gospel.

(1) Both Paul's description of the gospel as "the mystery of Christ" (v 4) and his own example (v 14-19) underline the vital importance of prayer for effective proclamation of and growth in the gospel.

(2) The unity of people from diverse backgrounds in the church is a witness to the world of the uniqueness and effectiveness of the gospel, so promoting and encouraging unity is essential.

(3) The mystery of Christ is revealed through preaching the written word of God, so those who do not have this gift themselves should seek to help and support those who do (1 Peter 4 v 10-11)—by encouraging teachers and evangelists, by praying for them, by supporting them financially, by bringing people to hear the gospel or creating opportunities in the community for the gospel to be preached, by relieving evangelists and teachers of other duties, by helping church leaders ensure that gospel preaching remains a priority, by supporting the training of evangelists and teachers in the next generation, and so on.

(4) Evangelism often has to take place in the context of suffering (v 1, 13) so we should be ready both to suffer ourselves and to encourage, support and pray for others who suffer for the gospel.

12. APPLY: What have you learned about the importance of the church? God displays His wisdom—the wisdom of the gospel and salvation—through the church (v 10-11). We deny God His glory if we claim to be Christian, yet refuse to be known as part of Christ's new community.

- **What difference should that make in our discipleship and our outreach?** Joining a faithful, biblical local church and committing ourselves to serving our fellow Christians there should be a priority for every believer. And in our evangelism we should call upon those who repent and believe to also join Christ's people and be an active part of His body.

7 Ephesians 4 v 1-16
GROWING IN CHRIST

THE BIG IDEA

The people of Christ's new community are given gifts by Him to prepare all believers for works of service, so that the body of Christ can be built up into the unity of the Spirit and into maturity that displays the fullness of Christ.

SUMMARY

Paul continues outlining God's plan for the church. Two responsibilities of every believer are highlighted. One is that we must make every effort to keep the unity of the Spirit. The other is that we are to use the gifts given to the church by Christ to be equipped to serve one another so that the body of Christ can be built up.

Keeping the unity of the Spirit involves first of all understanding and then living out the calling we have received: to display God's glory and wisdom in the church— that miraculous unity of believers from different backgrounds. It also involves each of us growing in humility, gentleness and patience. And this unity is found in nothing more or less than the essential apostolic teaching of the gospel.

Growth in maturity is not a personal, private project of each Christian. God's primary plan for our spiritual growth is our involvement in acts of service that will build up the church. Unfortunately, our current Christian culture places emphasis on our "personal relationship with Jesus" and our "personal spiritual growth", turning us into consumers who go into the spiritual marketplace looking for solutions to our private needs. But in God's plan we are to be providers

of spiritual help and encouragement, not consumers. Christ provides us with prophets, evangelists, pastors and teachers, who use God's word to teach and equip us. It's then our responsibility to serve and encourage one another.

The main practical challenge of this session is the call for every Christian to be an active member of a church.

OPTIONAL EXTRA

Get your group to discuss (light-heartedly) a subject on which they are instructed to try and come to a united opinion. Choose whatever is most appropriate for your group eg: The best song currently in the charts? The best film of the last year/ decade? The best current TV programme? The best candidate for national dish? The best candidate for president/prime minister? If you have a very homogenous group you may possibly achieve a high level of agreement, but it's most likely that there will be irreconcilable differences of opinion. In some groups you may find that opinion splits largely along lines of gender, which part of the country people come from (eg: northerners vs southerners), age etc. This activity demonstrates how unusual unity is in the world, and the fact that if it occurs anywhere it is usually found among people of the same type. By contrast, the unity of the Spirit that Paul writes about in Ephesians 4 is the result of God's supernatural work, bringing together Jew and Gentile in the body of Christ.

GUIDANCE ON QUESTIONS
1. What advice would you give to

someone who asks how they can grow as a Christian? In this session we will see God's plan for growing His people in the Christian faith. Most importantly, growth takes place in the setting of the church, where the body of Christ is built up through God's people serving one another, which they are equipped to do through the teaching of those that Christ has gifted for this purpose. It will be interesting to see how much advice offered by your group involves participation, service and ministry in the local church, or whether instead people think that growth mostly depends on personal and private Bible reading, Bible study, prayer and devotions. Rather than correct or commend people's answers at this stage, simply list them for future reference, as this question will be reviewed later in the session (see question 11).

2. Summarise our responsibility to one another, outlined in these verses. The first responsibility that Paul lists here for the church at Ephesus is to preserve the unity of the church.

3. In light of the previous chapters, why do you think we are to do this? In the first three chapters of Ephesians Paul has talked about God's plan to bring all things under Christ as head (1 v 10), and about the church being the body of Christ (1 v 23) and one new humanity formed out of two (2 v 15-16). It follows logically that Paul would then stress unity in the church—it shows what Christ's people already are.

4. What kind of people must we become (v 2)? Find three characteristics.
1. We must be "completely humble". Nothing destroys the unity of a relationship or the church like pride. Pride is our deadliest foe.

2. We are commanded to be "gentle"—instead of sharp and prickly.
3. We are to be "patient", which means bearing with one another in love. We will without question sometimes find ourselves offended—that goes without saying when a bunch of sinners are gathered together under the same roof! The very fact that Paul includes these instructions is evidence that he assumes there will be the need in the church to tolerate one another.

• **How will we think and act differently as we grow in each of these characteristics?** *Humility:* Being humble involves being ready to admit fault if you have said or done something wrong (not just giving a formal apology), and being willing to seek forgiveness from others. *Gentleness:* Someone who is gentle applies a light touch when interacting with others, and avoids wounding or crushing them. Gentleness encourages people into a closer relationship rather than repelling them (think how hard it would be to hug a porcupine!). It requires thinking of what is helpful for others rather than relieving our own feelings or forcing our views on them. *Patience:* We are not to be rash with one another or have short fuses. Instead, we are to restrain our minds and emotions, our ability to avenge ourselves and to hold a grudge. Patience is a kind of mercy.

5. How are we to go about preserving unity? What do the following verses tell us?
• **v 1:** "Live a life worthy of the calling you have received". That calling is their oneness in Christ and the task of bringing glory to Christ through being unified.
• **v 3:** "Make every effort to keep the unity…" This suggests that preserving

unity won't be easy—it doesn't come naturally—but the saints at Ephesus are to spare no effort or expense in pursuing it.

- **v 4-6:** "There is one body and one Spirit … one hope … one Lord, one faith, one baptism; one God and Father of all". Paul lays stress on the things that are essential to making us Christians. It is doctrinal unity that he emphasises. He is not saying all Christians must feel the same way, or have the same kind of reaction to various issues, or have the same interests. Rather, the unity of Christ's people is a unity in the truth.

6. APPLY: "To unite or not to unite?" What are the two opposing errors that Christians must guard against when confronted with this question? The first error is to impose uniformity on Christians in the name of unity, and accuse anyone who is merely different of being divisive. It is clear from this passage that Christian unity is built on the essentials of the faith. Paul doesn't say we're to be one in our musical tastes, our preferences for the type of clothes we wear, or even our desire for a certain style of preaching or a particular teacher. The second error is to seek unity with those who do not share a belief in the essentials of the Christian faith. Christian unity is found in a common understanding of what it means to be a Christian as found in God's word. So we may know fine, church-going people, but if they have no understanding that Christ is the unique Son of God, fully God and fully man, through whose sacrifice we must be saved by grace through faith, or if they have no commitment to that truth, we must conclude that we don't both have one Lord and so we cannot be united. We may love them, but we are not of one faith.

- **Which are you most prone to fall into?**

And how can you avoid it? Often our personalities affect which error we are more susceptible to. Controlling types will be more attracted to uniformity in place of unity, whereas laid-back, tolerant types will fear that refusing to unite looks like judgmentalism. We can also be affected by past experiences—people who have been involved in a church that was derailed by false teaching may be fearful of uniting with others who are a bit different. Those who have suffered a church split may be anxious to avoid any division at all. But no decision to be united with or to divide from others should be based on these considerations—we must look to the essential teaching of the Christian faith. If others are committed to this then, as Christ's people together, we are commanded to make every effort to keep that unity.

EXPLORE MORE
Read the following passages and note how we can identify those with whom we should not unite:
Matthew 7 v 15-23: False prophets can be recognised by the fruit that they produce. There is a warning here that it is not safe to judge such people by words alone since these may sound good (v 22), or by miracles and exorcisms that they perform, since these are no guarantee of knowing Christ (see also Matthew 24 v 24). Christians should look for leaders and teachers whose lives display and are growing the fruit of the Spirit (Galatians 5 v 22-23).
Luke 6 v 26: We should be suspicious of Christian leaders and teachers who are highly regarded by everyone. The world opposes God's ways (Ephesians 2 v 2), so the approval of men of the world suggests the message is a worldly one, rather than God's truth. By contrast, faithful teaching

of the gospel will always provoke hostility in those who follow the ways of the world. **Galatians 1 v 8-9:** The gospel never alters, and anyone who teaches something different to the truth as written by Christ's apostles in the Bible, whether by addition or subtraction, is clearly a false teacher.

1 Timothy 6 v 3-5: An unhealthy interest in controversies and quarrels (v 4), and using Christian ministry for financial gain (v 5) are both marks of false teachers.

1 John 2 v 18-19: Leaving God's people is a sign that such people do not truly belong there, so we should beware of any leader who cuts himself off from a faithful Bible-believing church to set up his own group.

7. What responsibility to each other does Paul highlight in these verses (v 12-13; also v 16)? To serve the church for the purpose of building it up until it matures and reaches its fullness. Verse 16 underlines that "each part" of the church is to be involved in building up the "body of Christ" ie: all believers are to be involved in Christian service.

8. What goal is in view here (v 13-16)? The goal of God's people serving one another is expressed in several different ways. First, unity—in the faith and in the knowledge of the Son of God (v 13). Second, maturity ie: full of the fulness of Christ (v 13). The implication here must be that in this world there is always more maturity to be achieved. Third, growing up into Christ, the Head (v 15). This picture combines both unity—as we become more united with Christ, and with each other in Christ—and maturity: the body becomes "grown up".

- **How will we know that the goal is being achieved (v 14-15)?** The mark of

a mature Christian is that they hold firmly to the gospel in all circumstances, and they are able to do that most difficult thing—to speak the truth in love (v 15).

9. What has Christ given to the church to bring this about (v 11)? Christ has given gifts of grace to each one of His people to equip God's people to serve and build up the church (v 12). Notice that Jesus has gifted people differently, but all these gifts are to "equip [God's] people for works of service".

- **What grounds do we have to be confident about how the church has been equipped (v 7-10)?** Christ is the one who equips His church. Verse 8 (quoting from Psalm 68) pictures Christ as a triumphant conqueror, distributing gifts to those who follow Him. In verses 9-10 Paul underlines that this is the same Christ whose life in this world was, by worldly standards, unimpressive, impoverished and obscure, ending in a torturous and humiliating death. The One who can "fill the whole universe" is supremely able to equip His people with all that we need to fulfil His purposes. We can trust Him to know what He's doing.

10. How do Christ's people become servants (v 11-12a)? In verses 11-12a Paul is not talking about the gifts as much as he is emphasising the people with the gifts: some to be apostles, some to be prophets, and so on. Jesus intends these people and their gifts to be used not for their popularity or personal benefit, but for the equipping of the saints. So Christians become servants by listening to and benefiting from the ministry of God's apostles—whose teaching is now written down in the New Testament—and of His prophets, evangelists, pastors and teachers, who use God's word to teach, rebuke, correct and train God's people in righteousness (2 Timothy 3 v 16).

11. APPLY: In light of what you have learned in this session, would you adjust your advice to the Christian who wants to grow in faith (Question 1)? How?
God's primary plan for our spiritual growth is our involvement in acts of service that will build up the church—that we live the faith out together as one. It is not fundamentally about having regular, personal, private quiet times (which are not commanded anywhere in Scripture). If that sounds weird to us, it's because our current Christian culture places so much emphasis on our "personal relationship with Jesus" and our "personal spiritual growth". And our culture teaches us to be consumers who go out into the spiritual marketplace looking for solutions to our private needs and wants. But you are not a consumer but a provider. It's just like God to plan our blessing by turning us away from ourselves and outward in service to our brothers and sisters. If you're not growing, ask yourself whether it's because you are not connected to the body of Christ and serving others as you ought.

• **How should we apply this to ourselves?** We all need to be active, serving members of a group of Christians. We need to add corporate Bible teaching, Bible study and prayer to our own quiet times. That means making the teaching meetings a priority; making sure you go regularly to a church prayer meeting; being willing to contribute in a Bible-study and doing any preparation needed; talking to others at church about what you have heard from the Bible and how it applies; looking out for those who need helping or encouraging, and being ready to accept encouragement/advice from others.

12. APPLY: What will it mean for us to speak the truth in love (v 15)? Depending on our personalities and backgrounds, we tend to fall off on one side or the other. We either speak the truth with very little love or we're full of what we think is love for others without telling them the truth. However, to have the truth and not speak it is not love (Proverbs 27 v 5). And to speak the truth without doing it in love makes you "only a resounding gong or a clanging cymbal" (1 Corinthians 13 v 1). Allow the group to discuss what practical steps need to be taken for them to speak the truth in love to one another, or use the headings below to stimulate discussion:
1. Speak spiritually: We need to give ourselves to talking more often about spiritually important things instead of the latest football game, fishing trip, television show, or community hearsay.
2. Know what the truth is: This is why we need God's gifts to the church of teachers.
3. Have close relationships: How will our words matter if we are not meaningfully united with each other in the fellowship?
4. Take responsibility for helping others spiritually: We need to have a concern that others won't mature if we don't help them.
5. Grow in humility, gentleness and patience: Without these qualities our words will cause division and strife.
6. Accept truth spoken in love to us: How will I conquer pride if no one points it out to me? How will I grow in patience if those around me don't lovingly speak to me about the ways they see impatience in my life? And how can I expect people to listen to me if I don't listen to them?

8

Ephesians 4 v 17 – 5 v 17

CLOTHED WITH NEW LIFE

THE BIG IDEA

The people of Christ's new community have their minds renewed through the apostles' teaching about the truth of Jesus Christ, so that they can put off the old self and instead put on the new self, created to be like God in true righteousness and holiness.

SUMMARY

Paul has been arguing that unity and maturity in the Christian church grow out of the work of God in saving sinners and making them one new humanity and one body (Ephesians 1 – 3). Chapter 4 has begun the section of the letter that sets out how we live out the theological truths of chapters 1 – 3.

In verses 17-24 Paul draws a bright and broad distinction between the Ephesians' past lives as Gentiles and their new lives in Christ. Verses 17-19 remind the Gentile Christians of what a ruined life looks like. Paul insists that they must no longer live that way. Instead, they must recognise that the new life of Christ is entirely different from the life of sin. Paul's vivid image of "putting off" the old self and "putting on" the new self teaches us that there is a spiritual "dress code" for the people of God.

The transformation of a believer from the old way of life to the new comes about through the apostles' teaching of the truth that is in Christ—teaching that today comes to us through the written word of God. Four things are mentioned here that Christ's people need to be taught: the truth about Jesus, how to put off the old self, about how our minds are renewed (the work of the Spirit through the gospel) and how to

put on the new self. The rest of these verses give us practical examples of how we put off the old and put on the new. Paul outlines "new clothes" for the mouth, the hands, and the heart.

This session looks at the relationship between faith and action, and between God's part and our part in the process of growing to be more like Christ. We are challenged to make hearing and learning from the teaching of God's word a priority, and to think about how we can be helped and also help others to put on the new clothes of life in Christ.

Note: Ephesians 5 v 1-17 is covered in Explore More.

OPTIONAL EXTRA

Corporations which are concerned about their image often have dress codes. Often a dress code is meant to convey a certain image to outsiders. In other cases, it is a matter of practicality, enabling workers to do their job more efficiently. If relevant, ask people to explain the dress code that applies in their particular occupation or company. Alternatively, pass round some pictures of people from different professions and discuss what message is given out by their clothing. What clothing would be considered unsuitable, and why?

GUIDANCE ON QUESTIONS

1. How do people change when they come to faith in Jesus Christ? If you know the people in your group are Christians, you could rephrase this question as follows: How do you think you have changed since you came to faith in Jesus Christ? If you are not sure whether people in your group are Christians, this may be one way to find out, as non-Christians often will not be able to pinpoint any profound turnabout in their lives, whereas a true Christian always will (see Ephesians 2 v 1-4; 11-13; 19-20; 4 v 17-24), even if that change has taken place over a long period. Alarm bells should ring if someone says something like: "My parents had me baptised, so I've always been a Christian" or "I've always been a good person". If the people in your group are non-Christians, they may be able to talk about others who have become Christians and whose lives they have seen change. Be prepared for some non-Christians to express these changes in negative terms ("They're always quoting the Bible at me." "We never go out and get drunk any more.").

2. What does Paul insist on here (v 17)?
They are to stop living like unbelievers, pagans and heathens. In the original language the words of verse 17 are strong and escalating. Paul says: "I tell you this…" and then adds: "and insist on it." And if that were not enough, he calls on the authority of the Lord to support his teaching.

3. How do the Gentiles live (v 17-19)? What is said about…
- **their minds?** The problem with the Gentiles' way of life doesn't begin with what they do—it begins with their futile and darkened thinking. Their living is wrong because their thinking is wrong.

- **their spiritual condition?** Regardless of whether they know it or care about it, they are now dead in their sins.

- **their consciences?** They have lost all sensitivity. They've lost the capacity to feel shame, which would have restrained their behaviour.

- **their behaviour?** They are overcome by their desires, which they seek to satisfy without restraint. (See Romans 1 v 28-32.)

4. Why do they live this way (v 18)?
Their problem is not innocence but ignorance. Many people confuse the two. Instead of being innocent they are culpable, responsible and guilty because of their ignorance. So their ignorance is willful—it is "due to the hardening of their hearts". They don't want to hear, believe and respond to the truth, but prefer to chase after the vanities of sin.

5. What is the only alternative to the Gentiles' way of life (v 20-21)? Knowing Christ (v 20). Paul describes the message about Him as "the truth that is in Jesus" (v 21). This is a claim of exclusivity—if something is "the truth", then anything different cannot be the truth. There are only two ways to live: as an unbeliever destined to hell, or as one who has received the salvation of the Lord and has been changed by God.

6. How did the Ephesians change from one way of life to the other? Find four things that they were taught.
- **v 21:** They heard about Jesus and were taught the truth that is in Him. Without Jesus there is no salvation and only ignorance, impurity and separation from God. The truth about Jesus is the foundation of all other teaching in the church.

- **v 22:** But they were also taught to put off the old way of life. Christians need to be taught what is wrong about the old way of life and how they must give up those things.

- **v 23:** They were taught about being

made new in the attitude of their minds. It doesn't make sense to change from dirty clothes to clean, fresh ones, without cleaning up. So, Paul says take off the old self and then be cleansed, have your mind renewed. But notice the words are passive, which means this is something that must be done to us. Paul has in mind the sanctifying work of the Holy Spirit, who renews us in the inner man.

• **v 24:** They were taught a new way to live—to put on the new self. Christians need to know the characteristics and ways of living that are appropriate for a Christian, and to be challenged to live in this way.

7. APPLY: What's the relationship between faith (the Christian's response to the truth that is in Jesus) and action (the Christian's response to teaching about putting off the old self and putting on the new self)? Christians have been saved by faith alone: the truth about Jesus is that He has done everything needed for us to be saved, and there is nothing for us to do except to put our trust in Him. But although we are saved by faith alone, the faith that saves is never alone. The metaphor Paul uses for this is one of changing our clothes (v 22, 24). In other words, faith is not just intellectual acceptance of the truth about Jesus; it requires our action—changing the way we live so that our lives fit with the truth about Jesus (see James 2 v 14-26). The root of our salvation is faith in Jesus Christ but the fruit is a changed life.

• **What is God's part and what is our part?** *God's part:* Through the gospel God enlightens the eyes of our heart (compare 1 v 18), gives us a renewed mind (4 v 23) and provides the "new clothes" that will make us like God (v 24).

Our part: Christians should not sit around doing nothing while waiting for God to transform us. We need to take off the old self and put on the new self—to reject the way in which we lived when we were ignorant, to think with the renewed mind that God has given us, and to do the things that we are taught that make us like God in righteousness and holiness. We must put the new clothes on.

8. APPLY: What should we expect a good church to teach? Base this answer on the four points covered in question 6 above. Help your group to think about the sort of things they can expect to hear from a church that teaches faithfully, and also think about the kind of teaching that is inadequate.

Teaching about Jesus: Teaching about God alone is not sufficient. Without knowing the truth about Jesus, no one can give up the old way of life.

Teaching about change: The change from the old self to the new self is something that is taught. There is a damaging tendency in some churches to think that all we need to do is get someone to "pray the prayer" and then we can leave them to themselves. But Jesus says: "Go and make disciples … teaching them to obey everything that I have commanded" (Matthew 28 v 19-20).

Teaching about putting off the old self: We must love each other enough to get into each other's business, to tell each other where we are going wrong, and to insist that we take off the old self and put on the new. So we should expect to hear teaching that is negative, that rebukes and then corrects—not out of self-righteousness or control-freakery or with a judgmental attitude, but with love for each other and a desire to see our fellowship be like Jesus.

Teaching about the renewed mind: We should expect to hear something very different from mere morality or the power of positive thinking ie: how to be a good person, how to turn our lives around. We should be left in no doubt that every person needs—and in Christ can receive—the supernatural power of God at work within us through His Spirit.

Teaching about putting on the new self: We need to know in practical ways what the new self looks like, and not assume that people know what it is to be righteous. The world in its ignorance has its own interpretations of goodness and righteousness, which are often at variance with God's ways. We need to put on the new clothes that God has provided and not shoddy fakes.

- **We've seen that Christians need to be taught how to put off the old self and put on the new self. How should the importance of this teaching affect our involvement in our church?** We should do all we can to make sure we benefit from the good teaching (eg: ask a more mature Christian about things we don't understand; spend time thinking and praying about the Bible passage during the week; talk to others after the meeting about what we've just heard, with the aim of encouraging one another).

9. How will we look in our "new clothes"? For instance...

- **How will we / how won't we speak (v 25, 29)?** We are to speak truth and not lies (v 25). We are to say things that build others up and avoid saying things that are unwholesome—meaning we should say nothing crass, unclean or unkind; no cursing, gossip, slander and so on (v 29).
- **What will we do, and not do, with our hands (v 28)?** We are to stop stealing and instead work and do something useful

with our hands. This is not merely for our own good—like our speech, our hands are to help and build up those in need. They are clothed with the gloves of charity and service. Note: Here is a good principle for career selection: do what seems most useful for advancing the glory of God and serving others, given your abilities and gifts.

- **How will we, and how won't we, respond in our hearts when something makes us angry (v 26-27, 31-32)?** We are told not to sin in our anger—we need to resolve our anger before the day ends (v 26). In other words, don't be comfortable with anger because over time it will become bitterness and resentment, and produce the "fruit" listed in v 31. Don't believe the temptation that tells you that it's good and empowering to hold on to some of your anger. Don't give in to thinking that you know how to act justly in your anger. We wear the clothing of a new heart by resolving anger quickly, before it grows into evil action and a hardened heart (v 31).

⌄

- **What does Paul appeal to in persuading us to be kind, compassionate and forgiving (v 32)?** He points out that in Christ God forgave each of us. In Christ's crucifixion, God forgives those who repent and believe. That's our model for forgiving one another.

10. Who is affected by our failure or refusal to put on our new clothes (v 30)?
Paul says: "Do not grieve the Holy Spirit of God". Our lives affect the heart of God Himself. Lying, stealing, sinful anger etc. pull apart what the Holy Spirit binds together. So

when we hurt Christ's body, the church, we grieve the Holy Spirit as well. Reverence for the Holy Spirit should prevent us from living like pagans.

EXPLORE MORE

Read Ephesians 5 v 1-17 ... What old clothes and new clothes does Paul add here? Old clothes: sexual immorality, impurity and greed (v 3); obscenity, foolish talk, coarse joking (v 4). New clothes: sacrificial love like Christ's (v 2); thanksgiving (v 4); goodness, righteousness and truth (v 9).

How does he sum up our new life in Christ (v 2, 8, 15)? And the old life (v 5, 6, 15 and 17)? "A life of love" (v 2), "light in the Lord" (v 8) and "wise" (v 15). The old life is summed up as idolatry (v 5), disobedience (v 6) and foolishness (v 15, 17).

What reasons does he give that should motivate us to live out our new life in Christ (v 2, 5-6, 16)? Positively we are motivated to put on our new clothes by the sacrificial love of Christ (v 2) and negatively by the promise of God's wrath on those who continue to live lives of disobedience (v 6). But we should also understand God's plan to bring everything under Christ (1

v 10), and the role of His people in bringing that about—by making the most of every opportunity to bring the light of Christ to the lives of those around us still in darkness (v 16, compare Colossians 4 v 5)

What action do we need to take (v 1, 6, 10, 16, 17)? Christians put off the old self and put on the new as they seek to be imitators of God (v 1), as they guard against being deceived (v 6), as they find out what pleases the Lord (v 10) and understand what His will is (v 17), and as they make the most of every opportunity to display Christ in their lives (v 16). Notice again how crucial it is to receive faithful and accurate teaching.

11. APPLY: What would most encourage you to put on the new self?
• **What can you do to encourage the same in others?**
Give your group a minute or so in which they can write down one practical thing that would most help them to live as Christ's people in the ways that have been mentioned and discussed in Q10, as well as one thing that they think they could do to help other Christians in the same way. Then get people to share what they have written before you pray together.

---

9 Ephesians 5 v 18 – 6 v 9
FILLED WITH THE SPIRIT

THE BIG IDEA
When Christ's new community is filled with the Spirit, He controls our minds and transforms our behaviour, so that the grace of God and the love of Christ are on display in our everyday actions and relationships.

SUMMARY
Paul continues to apply the truths of the gospel to our everyday lives. Having contrasted the old life of sin with the new life of Christ, he now commands the Ephesians to be filled with the Spirit, and

sets out what a Spirit-filled life looks like. Paul lists four characteristics of the Spirit-filled person. They are:

1. Speaking to one another with psalms, hymns and spiritual songs.
2. Singing and making music in your heart to the Lord.
3. Giving thanks to God for everything.
4. Submitting to one another out of reverence for Christ.

In all these actions characteristic of a Spirit-filled life, we're ultimately concerned with loving and honouring the Lord Jesus. A Spirit-filled life is a Christ-centred life.

This emphasis on behaviour may be surprising for some, who equate being filled with the Spirit with an experience or power that overwhelms a person mentally, emotionally and even physically. By contrast, Paul highlights the actions of a Spirit-filled person—things that we consciously decide to do and ways in which we consciously decide to relate to God and others. People who do the things Paul lists here show that they are filled with the Spirit. People who don't do these things show they are not filled with the Spirit, regardless of the experiences they claim or the emotions they display in public meetings. The fact that Paul commands us to be filled with the Spirit is significant because you cannot command someone to feel an emotion or be taken over by an experience; you can only command people to do things.

Finally Paul focuses on three areas of life —marriage, parenting and work (slaves/ employees and masters/employers)—to show us what godly submission and godly authority, characteristics of Spirit-filled people, look like in our daily relationships. Godly submission and authority are modelled on the relationship between Christ and His people. As Spirit-filled people relate

to each other in the ways described here, we put on display to the whole world the grace of God in Christ and the love of Christ for His people.

OPTIONAL EXTRA

Use a whiteboard, flipchart or overhead projector and write two headings: "Authority" and "Submission". Find out what people in your group associate with these words (or what you think most people would associate with them) and make a list under each heading. At the end of the session you can review this, and perhaps make two new, alternative lists, in light of what you have learned from the Bible. (Link this to Question One.)

GUIDANCE ON QUESTIONS

1. How do you feel about authority? What do you think when you hear the word "authority"? In western culture it is common to view authority very negatively or, at best, as a necessary evil. Authority is seen as an enemy of freedom (defined as no restraint, no limits, and no responsibility). You could ask the following question: Is there any relationship between authority and love? It will be interesting to see whether people think of them as "close friends" or "feuding strangers". This session describes what it means to be Spirit-filled and how people filled with the Spirit conduct themselves in everyday relationships of authority and submission. We'll see that authority modelled on Christ's headship of the church is very different from how the world views authority.

2. What is prohibited in verse 18? And what is commanded? We are told not to get drunk on wine. (Note that Paul is not addressing all drinking of alcohol, but drunkenness.) Instead we are commanded to be filled with the Holy Spirit. What a contrast! It's amazing how paltry this world's idea of the good life is when compared to what's available to the Christian—literally "be continuously and repeatedly filled/controlled with the Spirit". That's the main idea of this verse.

3. Paul deliberately contrasts being drunk with being filled with the Holy Spirit. What one effect on people do they have in common? Although being drunk and being filled with the Spirit lead to completely opposite outcomes, the one effect that they have in common is control of our minds, resulting in a dramatic transformation in behaviour. Just as alcohol takes over control of our mental faculties, causing us to do foolish, shameful and even dangerous things, so being filled with the Spirit means being controlled by the third Person of the Trinity, and the result is also a transformation in the way we live.

4. What does drunkenness lead to?
Debauchery—failing to exercise any self restraint when it comes to satisfying our lustful desires. Debauchery results in excessive squandering of money, energy, time, talents and opportunities, finally ending in a wasted life.

5. What does being filled with the Spirit lead to? To show us what Spirit-filled living looks like in the church, Paul lists four characteristics of the Spirit-filled person. They are (1) Speaking to one another with psalms, hymns and spiritual songs. (2) Singing and making music in your heart to the Lord. (3) Giving thanks to God for everything. (4) Submitting to one another out of reverence for Christ.
Instead of a list of different instructions, verses 18-21 are really one long sentence in the original. We know that someone is filled with the Spirit when they do these other things.

6. Look at the characteristics of a Spirit-filled person. What does each mean in practice?
• **v 19a:** "[Speak] to one another with … songs": This is congregational singing—singing together as a church; not watching others sing but participating. As we do this, we speak to each other the truths expressed in the song. We teach, instruct, admonish and encourage one another as we sing. Maybe this is why we're really encouraged when we have a good music day, or when we sing those songs where we all seem to be into it.

⌄

• **What are the implications for the kinds of songs we should sing together?** The words are important. We need to guard against being swept away by a good tune while singing words that are merely sentimental or even biblically incorrect. We need to choose songs that express the truth and whose words can teach, instruct, admonish and encourage us.

• **v 19b:** "Sing … to the Lord": Our singing has a vertical dimension as well as a horizontal one. Not only do Spirit-filled people speak to others in psalms, hymns, and spiritual songs, but we also speak to the Lord. Singing mechanically without engaging our minds and hearts is a sign that we are not letting the Spirit control our mind.

• **v 20:** "Always giving thanks": Instead of constantly expressing grumbles, stress or gloom, a Spirit-filled person is always thankful to the Father for everything.

- **v 21:** "Submit to one another": The Spirit-filled life is one marked by submission to others—ordering your life under another's for their benefit. This is the principle that underlies instructions like 4 v 29, 31-32.

⊻

- **What are the implications here for, say, our music preferences in church?** The Spirit unites Christ's people in Him (4 v 3). You see, then, how ridiculous it is for churches to argue, fight, and even split over something like music styles. Paul lists here psalms, hymns, and spiritual songs. There is room for variety, and that variety will exalt Christ if we're Spirit-filled. The more mature Christian will delight at one more opportunity to make music to Jesus in his heart, and is happy to submit to other believers. They can say: "That song wouldn't be my preference, but I know that half the congregation loves it and is drawn to Christ by it, so I'm happy to submit to them and to speak to them in song to encourage and build them up."

7. What's the connection in these verses between the Spirit and Christ? As we sing and make music in our hearts, it's "to the Lord". As we give thanks to God the Father in everything, it's "in the name of our Lord Jesus Christ". And as we submit to one another, we do so "out of reverence for Christ". A Spirit-filled life is a Christ-centred life. This shouldn't surprise us—Jesus Himself said that this would be the role of the Spirit (John 15 v 26). Being controlled by God the Holy Spirit means we honour Christ's authority.

8. APPLY: How is Paul's description of a Spirit-filled person different from **what you expected, or from other ideas you have heard about being Spirit-filled?** Many people equate being filled with the Spirit with an experience or power that overwhelms a person mentally, emotionally and even physically, resulting in crying, laughing, shouting out, falling down, speaking in tongues or making animal noises. By contrast, Paul's description of a Spirit-filled person doesn't mention any of these things; instead he highlights the actions of a Spirit-filled person—things that we consciously decide to do and ways in which we consciously decide to relate to God and others. Also notice that Paul commands us to be filled with the Spirit. This is significant because you cannot command someone to feel an emotion or be taken over by an experience; you can only command people to do things.

- **How can we know if someone is a Spirit-filled person?** By what they do, or don't do. A Spirit-filled person will sing in church meetings with an attitude of gratitude to God and a desire to encourage others. They will be thankful, not complaining, and submissive to the interests of others because of their reverence for the Lord, not selfish and rebellious, or resentful and grudging in their service of others. People who don't do these things are not filled with the Spirit, regardless of the experiences they claim or the emotions they display in public meetings. Above all, a Spirit-filled person will be Christ-centred. Ironically, someone who only ever talks about the Spirit and never mentions Christ demonstrates that they are not filled with the Spirit.

EXPLORE MORE
... Read Titus 3 v 4-7; Ephesians 1 v 13-14. **How does the New Testament answer these questions [about who has**

the Spirit; when Christians receive the Spirit; whether all Christians have the Spirit]?

Titus 3 v 4-7: When someone repents and believes in Jesus, God pours out on them the Holy Spirit, who gives new life—"rebirth" and "renewal" (see also John 3 v 3-8).

Ephesians 1 v 13-14: All who are in Christ have received the Spirit as a seal (showing God's ownership of us) and as a deposit guaranteeing our inheritance—and that continues until our future redemption. It's clear from these passages that all Christians receive the Spirit when they are saved and continue to have the Spirit until Christ's return. There is no such thing as a Christian who does not have the Spirit.

Read Galatians 5 v 25; Ephesians 4 v 30. Do all Christians benefit equally from the Spirit? In Gal 5 v 25, those who "live by the Spirit" (= have been saved and born again) are commanded to "keep in step with the Spirit" (= live in obedience to what the Spirit wants). (Note: Be aware that "live" in v 16 means to live in obedience to the Spirit ie: it has a different meaning to "live" in v 25. The ESV is a clearer translation.)

Where does Paul's command to be filled with the Spirit fit in? Ephesians 4 v 30 shows that it is possible for Christians, who all have the Spirit, to grieve Him by not obeying Him. To summarise, all Christians have the Spirit, but not all will benefit equally from Him because of the disobedience of some. We can now see that Paul's command to "be filled with the Spirit" in 5 v 18 is a command, not to receive the Spirit, but to obey Him.

9. Fill in the table. Notice how Paul links behaviour with truth about Christ. See answers in the table over the page.

Note: In the following Apply section, try to

concentrate on the areas that are of specific importance to your group, and make the connection with Christ, rather than making the application moralistic. If the group needs to go into detail, plan a separate session to unpack these roles and relationships. Use the question to make sure people understand clearly what Paul is teaching in these verses, and then encourage them to think about what they might need to change in their own lives. If only one of these categories is applicable to your group, concentrate on that category.

10. APPLY: What does marriage in particular show us about Christ and how should this affect the way that wives and husbands relate to each other? The apostle Paul discloses a "profound mystery", which is that in a truly Christian marriage, as described in 5 v 22-33, the relationship between Christ and the church is revealed. The world doesn't understand what church is or Christ's relationship with His people, but the world does recognise what a good marriage is. Christian marriages can show that love and authority, respect and submission belong together. Because marriage is a parable of the gospel, when Christian husbands refuse to love and lead or Christian wives refuse to respect and submit, we obscure or demean the truth about Jesus and the church, about His sacrificial love and death for His people, and their submission to Him. Christians must never give up on marriages because more is at stake than our temporary circumstances or desires. This is why the main battlefield the devil has chosen for his warfare has always been marriage. Believers need to keep praying for Christian marriages—that Christ may be plainly seen in them.

Wives: The command to submit to your husband literally means to order yourself

Verses	Who?	What's the command?	How? (Link with Christ)	Why?
5 v 22-24	Wives	Submit to your husbands	As to the Lord (v 22)	Husband = head of the wife, just as Christ = head of church (v 23)
5 v 25-32	Husbands	Love your wives	As Christ loved the church (v 25) ie: sacrificially	Marriage is a picture of Christ and the church (v 32)
6 v 1-3	Children	Obey your parents	In the Lord (v 1)	1. This is right (v 1) 2. That it may go well with you (v 3)
6 v 4	Fathers	1. Don't exasperate your children 2. Train and instruct them in the Lord	Train and instruct them in the Lord	
6 v 5-8	Slaves	Obey your masters respectfully and sincerely (v 5), and wholeheartedly (v 7)	As if you were serving the Lord (v 7)	The Lord will reward you (v 8)
6 v 9	Masters	Treat your slaves well and don't threaten them	"In the same way" (see slaves, v 5) = as if serving the Lord	You have a Master in heaven who does not show favouritism (v 9)

under your husband. But Paul draws a parallel between wives and husbands, and the church and Christ. Since Christ's headship is supreme and universal (1 v 10, 22; 4 v 15-16) the implication of this, spelled out by Paul in verse 24, is that wives should submit to their husbands in everything.

Note: Paul is setting out the pattern for Christian marriage here and not dealing with problems such as marriage to an unbeliever or what to do if a husband wants his wife to sin. However, it's likely that some in your group will raise these difficulties. For instructions on these issues see 1 Peter 3 v 1-2; Titus 2 v 5.

Husbands: The husband is not told to be the head of his wife—he is the head already. It's a statement of fact, not a command. All that remains is whether he will be a good (ie: Christ-like) head or not. A Christ-like head in marriage will love his wife "as Christ loved the church" which means…

(1) Giving himself up for her. Christian husbands are called to sacrificial love.

(2) Aiming to help his wife become more radiant and beautiful (because she has grown in holiness, 5 v 26-27) than when he first married her. Treating his wife as he would his own body absolutely rules out physical threats or abuse. Husbands are to

love their wives in such a way as to make independence a burden and submission a joy.

11. APPLY: What does Paul's teaching here mean for...

- **children?** Again, concentrate on the category most applicable to your group. If most people in your group are neither children or fathers, focus the discussion on how to encourage children and fathers in your church to act rightly.

  Children are to obey their parents. Compare the fifth commandment, to honour your parents, which has no age restriction—as adults we are to honour our parents even when we no longer have to obey them. Obedience to parents means to respond immediately without complaining and with joy. And it's your parents you are to obey, not your friends or other significant role-models; parents are the authority that God has placed in your life. Finally, you are to obey them in the Lord—that is, as long as they are not asking you to sin. In the west, godly obedience to parents means that Christian young people must resist the surrounding culture that seeks to pull them away from the influence of their parents.

- **fathers?** It is the responsibility of fathers to attend to their children's spiritual welfare. This means fathers are not to exercise authority for its own sake or for their own comfort and convenience—that is what exasperates children and young people. Fathers are to exercise their authority, not by yelling, abusing, berating or condemning—but by training (coaching, practising, modelling how to think and live) and by teaching (talking, asking questions, sharing knowledge, having devotions together). Fathers shouldn't be afraid to say no to the world, the culture,

their child or their child's friends. That's a father's role, responsibility and right, and it is a great act of love to do so. Dads may need to ask themselves: how can I teach and train if I never spend time with my children or talk with them about anything meaningful?

12. APPLY: What does Paul's teaching here mean for...

- **workers? Note:** Slaves in the New Testament world had some rights and privileges; they were often skilled labourers; and sometimes considered part of the family. We might apply Paul's instructions to slaves to employees who serve in the workplace.

  Christians are to obey their employers as they would obey Christ. Employers should be beating down the doors of every church looking for Christian employees to work for them because it's common knowledge that Christians work as if they're working for Jesus. Some questions for workers to think about: Would you do the things you do at work if the Lord was there as your boss? Is your obedience total when your employers are not around? What things would you keep doing, stop doing, or change?

- **bosses?** "Treat your slaves in the same way"—that is, as if serving the Lord (see v 5). Christian bosses are to ensure the welfare of their workers, knowing they will give an account to God for how they treat a person made in God's image. "Do not threaten them"— rather, you should encourage, teach, and correct your workers. Don't play favourites because God doesn't.

10 Ephesians 6 v 10-24
READY FOR BATTLE

THE BIG IDEA

Christ's new community is at war with worldly powers and the spiritual forces of evil, but Christ our Commander is victorious and we have the armour of God to protect us.

SUMMARY

The apostle begins this section of the letter with the word "finally". But this "finally" is not a casual conclusion. In one sense, Paul has been building to this point all along—verses 10-20 restate and amplify all that has been said before this.

Paul has told us that the church is the centrepiece of God's activity in the universe. In Christ, the church will have all things put under its feet (1 v 22-23), and the church is to be the means of our practical holiness and growth in Christ-likeness, so that together we display the wisdom of God (3 v 10) and the love of Christ (4 v 32). Christianity is corporate—a person who becomes a Christian joins a "team", and this shapes every area of our lives.

Since the church lives for now in a world defined by disobedience and hostility to God (2 v 1-2), it's not surprising that Paul warns us that the church is at war against the forces of evil, both spiritual and worldly. Christians therefore need a wartime fighting mentality. But with the church at the centre of God's purposes, how can the final outcome of this war be in any doubt? In Christ and dressed in the armour of God, we have all the strength we need, not only to fight this war but to win it. We are strong—but only in the Lord's almighty power.

Spiritual warfare simply means putting on God's armour and taking our stand. We don't need to do any more against the enemy because Christ Himself has already fought and won the war on our behalf. Understanding this should make us people of prayer, looking to the Lord for our strength, united in concern to build up Christ's people in Him and to encourage one another.

GUIDANCE ON QUESTIONS

1. What do you think is the main reason why many Christians pray so little and so rarely? The purpose of this question is not to deal with all the issues at this point but to lead people to see how prayerlessness is a symptom of self-reliance—we don't pray because deep down we think we don't really need God. We fall into self-reliance because we don't properly appreciate our helplessness without God (remind people of Ephesians 2 v 1), or the ferocity of the spiritual war that is being waged over our souls. This session shows that in this world the church exists in a state of war, but that in Christ (and only in Him) we have total victory over God's enemies.

2. Summarise the situation that the church faces in this world. What does this mean for our lives as Christians? The church is at war. Since the church is God's way to reveal His wisdom (3 v 10-11) and the place where all things are brought under the feet of Christ (1 v 22-23), and since all this take places in a world defined by disobedience and hostility to God (2 v 1-2), it's inevitable that we will be attacked. This means that as Christians we need a wartime, fighting mentality.

3. What do we learn about our opponent (v 11-12)? We are not at war with flesh and blood (v 12). Whatever happens in the troubles and struggles that erupt between nations or men, we need to realise that those things are not where the real battle lies. Rather, we wrestle with the rulers, authorities and powers of this dark world and against the spiritual forces of evil in the heavenly realm. Our battle is spiritual and our opponent is a spiritual being—the devil (v 11), who is described as scheming against us.

4. Where does strength for this battle come from, and how do we get this for ourselves (v 10-11)? Our strength comes from the Lord (v 10). The good news is that we are called to battle against the devil in God's "mighty power", not in our own feebleness. We are, however, told to put on the full armour of God (v 11). So that's how we become strong in the Lord, by putting on God's armour. (Note: Verse 11 could also be understood as putting on God Himself.)

5. What can we then do against this opponent (v 11, 13, 14)? Four times in these few verses Paul exhorts Christians to "stand". In spiritual warfare, that is all we're called to do—to get dressed in God's armour and to stand. Be aware that some people may have seen, heard and read a lot of confusing things about spiritual warfare (eg: that it involves casting out demons, identifying and exorcising the sins of your ancestors, marching round physical territory to claim it, etc). But the Bible only tells us to put on the full spiritual armour—and then take our stand.

- **Why do you think we are commanded to do only this and not more?** Christians are to "stand" rather than to "advance" or "invade" because the

victory has already been won by Christ. Satan is already defeated (see Hebrews 2 v 14-15; Genesis 3 v 15), and so the battle is not ours to win. Instead we're to be like a Roman soldier standing at our post, defending the territory already won.

6. APPLY: Look at Paul's description of the Christian's spiritual armour (v 14-17). For each piece, what does it mean in practice to put it on? And what would it look like if you neglected to put it on? Notice that Paul twice says: "Put on the full armour of God". Wearing only some parts of God's armour but not others leaves vital limbs and organs uncovered and exposed to the enemy. If we're not wearing the whole armour, we're not properly dressed for battle!

- **The belt of truth (v 14):** One of the key strategies of the devil is to deceive. We need to know and keep learning God's truth to protect ourselves from the devil's lies. See 2 Corinthians 11 v 3-4.

- **The breastplate of righteousness (v 14):** Another key strategy of the devil is to remind Christians of their sin and bring them again under a sense of God's condemnation (Romans 7 v 21-24). The antidote is the New Testament teaching that Christ bears our sins and shares His righteousness with us (2 Corinthians 5 v 21). Clothed with the righteousness of Jesus Christ, we are no longer vulnerable to the devil's strategy of accusation and condemnation (Romans 8 v 1-4).

- **The "shoes" (ESV) of the gospel of peace (v 15):** The devil wants to see the church destroyed, not built up. If our feet are not fitted with the gospel of peace, we are not ready to grasp those opportunities the Lord gives us for spreading the gospel to others.

- **The shield of faith (v 16):** Faith is trust in God and His word—trusting that God is sovereign, faithful, good and gracious, trusting that His promises will never fail.

- **The helmet of salvation (v 17):** The hope of our full salvation on the day when Christ returns is what gives us peace, joy and patience in troubles and hardship, enabling Christ's people to persevere through every situation that the devil may throw at us.

- **The sword of the Spirit (v 17):** The word of God is the only offensive weapon we are given. For examples of how to use it, see Matthew 4 v 1-11 and Hebrews 4 v 12.

EXPLORE MORE

Read Isaiah 11 v 5; 52 v 7; 59 v 17. What are the parallels with the description of the armour of God in Ephesians 6?

11 v 5: The promised Messiah will wear the belt of righteousness (compare the belt of truth and the breastplate of righteousness in the armour of God).

52 v 7: This verse mentions the beautiful feet of those who bring the good news of the return of the LORD and the salvation of His people (compare the shoes (ESV) of readiness to spread the gospel in Eph 6).

59 v 17: God puts on a breastplate of righteousness and the helmet of salvation as He comes to redeem His people (v 20).

7. In verse 18 what do we learn about the final piece of God's armour—prayer.

- **How are we to pray?** "In the Spirit", which is not a reference to a private prayer language or praying in tongues. It's prayer inspired by and guided by the Spirit, the One who gives us access to the Father in prayer (2 v 18) and who fills us or controls us (5 v 18). And we are to

pray with alertness, not falling asleep—in other words, remembering that we are in the middle of a war, so watchful for the attacks of the devil, for casualties among those around us, and for the Lord's guidance and, ultimately, His return (1 Thessalonians 5 v 1-6).

- **When?** We are told to pray "on all occasions" and to "always keep on praying". This is a full-time job. We are to be in a constant attitude of prayer.

- **What kinds of prayers are mentioned?** We are to pray "with all kinds of prayers and requests". There is nothing beyond the scope of prayer. ACTS—Adoration… Confession… Thanksgiving… Supplication (= requests for help)—is a useful acrostic for helping us to remember the different ways in which we should pray.

- **Who for?** Paul calls the Ephesians, and God calls us, to pray for all the Lord's people. This means all Christians everywhere, so we should regularly pray for other churches and Christians in other nations.

8. What do we learn about the quality of relationships between those mentioned in these closing verses of Paul's letter? And what is done to maintain those relationships? A number of things could be highlighted here. Though a leader and an apostle of Christ, Paul doesn't set himself apart from his struggles and weakness—he is completely open about his need for other Christians to pray for him. He knows he cannot stand in this spiritual struggle in his own strength, and he knows he needs other believers to serve him by praying for him so he too can be built up (4 v 12). It was also important for Paul to organise face-to-face meetings. Paul was away from the Ephesians but he was not far from their thoughts and hearts.

9. Look at Paul's personal prayer request (v 19-20). How does it compare with what you might ask people to pray for you in Paul's situation? At the time of writing this letter, Paul is "in chains" (v 20). This imprisonment is the result of his gospel ministry (3 v 1). We might expect Paul to ask that the Ephesians pray for his release. Instead, Paul's priority is to continue preaching the gospel, whatever the consequences, seen in his asking the Christians to pray that he would be given the right words to say and that he would be fearless in continuing to preach the gospel.

10. APPLY: What could you do to bring your prayers—both alone and together with other Christians—in line with Paul's teaching and example here? Rather than spending untold numbers of hours talking to friends about things we know we should pray about, we should set a time when we start praying and stick to it. Instead of promising to pray for something but then forgetting about it, we should stop and pray there and then. We should actively plan to pray—if we don't have a plan, we will not pray effectively.

11. APPLY: What could you do to strengthen your relationships with fellow Christians, both in your local church and beyond? At this point you could review some of the things that we have learned from this letter about Christ's people—the church (see Optional Extra below). One of the reasons Christians may be reluctant to commit themselves to a local church is because they view church as the world does—old-fashioned, irrelevant, dull, controlling etc—and they don't understand the centrality of the church in the plans of

God, as taught in the New Testament. If we share Paul's view of the church (eg: 1 v 3, 22-23; 2 v 4-6, 19-22; 3 v 6, 10-11; 4 v 11-16), our priority will be to serve one another, build one another up, respond to one another with humility, gentleness and patience, exhort one another in song, submit to one another, pray for and encourage one another.

OPTIONAL EXTRA: REVIEW

1. Get your group (in pairs?) to go through the whole letter and find every place where Paul uses the phrases "in/through/with Christ" or "in the Lord". They should make two lists: one of all the things that God has done or is doing "in Christ", and the other of all that Christ's people receive "in Christ". (Note: not every use of these phrases will fit into one or other list.) End by reminding your group of what we learned in the first session—that Christ's people have every spiritual blessing in Him—and discuss how the truths represented by the two lists should shape our lives.

2. Get your group to come up with a presentation that summarises all they have learned from Ephesians about the church. They can include something on how their personal view of the church has changed. They could produce a song, poem, rap, poster or fact-file, or create a drama eg:
- a chat show, interviewing the Ephesians believers and Paul, the writer
- a quiz show about Paul's teaching

You could devote a whole extra session to this activity, giving your group plenty of time to look through Ephesians and find the things that have really impacted them. This activity is well worth the effort because of the sense of achievement and understanding that it gives to people at the end of this series of Bible studies.

thegoodbook
COMPANY
Opening up the Bible

At The Good Book Company, we are dedicated to helping Christians and local churches grow. We believe that God's growth process always starts with hearing clearly what he has said to us through his timeless word—the Bible.

Ever since we opened our doors in 1991, we have been striving to produce resources that honour God in the way the Bible is used. We have grown to become an international provider of user-friendly resources to the Christian community, with believers of all backgrounds and denominations using our Bible studies, books, evangelistic resources, DVD-based courses and training events.

We want to equip ordinary Christians to live for Christ day by day, and churches to grow in their knowledge of God, their love for one another, and the effectiveness of their outreach.

Call us for a discussion of your needs or visit one of our local websites for more information on the resources and services we provide.

Your friends at The Good Book Company

UK & EUROPE
NORTH AMERICA
AUSTRALIA
NEW ZEALAND

thegoodbook.co.uk
thegoodbook.com
thegoodbook.com.au
thegoodbook.co.nz

0333 123 0880
866 244 2165
(02) 6100 4211
(+64) 3 343 2463

WWW.CHRISTIANITYEXPLORED.ORG
Our partner site is a great place for those exploring the Christian faith, with a clear explanation of the good news, powerful testimonies and answers to difficult questions.